TUPAC SHAKUR

TUPAC AMA

1971-

RU SHAKUR

1996

By the Editors of VIBe

Three Rivers Press • New York

Editor: Alan Light
Editorial Assistant: Margeaux Watson

Jacket & Design Consultant: Ellen Fanning
Design Assistant: Dwayne Shaw
Picture Editor: George Pitts
Photo/Art Assistant: Duane Pyous

President & CEO of VIBE: Keith T. Clinkscales

Published by Three Rivers Press, a division of Crown Publishers, Inc., 201 East 50th Street, New York, New York 10022. Member of the Crown Publishing Group.

Originally published in hardcover by Crown Publishers, Inc., in 1997.

Random House, Inc. New York, Toronto, London, Sydney, Auckland
www.randomhouse.com

THREE RIVERS PRESS and colophon are trademarks of Crown Publishers, Inc.

Printed in the United States of America

Library of Congress Cataloging-in-Publication Data
Tupac Shakur / by the editors of Vibe.
    1. Shakur, Tupac, 1971–1996.   I. Vibe.
ML420.S529T87   1997
782.42164'092–dc21
[B]   97-2175
                                  CIP
                                  MN

ISBN 0-609-80217-8

10   9   8   7   6

ACKNOWLEDGMENTS

Our deepest thanks to everyone at VIBE who helped make this book—and everything else—possible: Quincy Jones, Bob Miller, John Rollins, Gil Rogin, Rob Kenner, Carter Harris, Andréa M. Duncan, Joe Angio, Diane Cardwell, Jonathan Van Meter, Omoronke Idowu, Shani Saxon, Michael A. Gonzales, Henry Hample, Chiedo Nkwocha, Ryan Jones, Ayana Byrd, Emil Wilbekin, Mimi Valdés,

Ambassador Bönz Malone, Gary Koepke, Diddo Ramm, and Karla Radford.

At Crown Publishers: Steve Ross, Carol Taylor, and Lara Webb.

Invaluable help of many kinds came from Lori Earl, Talibah Stewart, George Pryce, Greg Howard, Cassandra Butcher, Fab 5 Freddy, Suzanne McElfresh, Sleuth,

Gerard from Dooable Arts, Sue Yoder, Dana Lixenberg, Jan Pitts, Maria Alomillo, Shawn Mortensen, and Reisig & Taylor.

Special thanks to our wise and tireless agent, Sarah Lazin.

And Karen Lee, thank you more than we can say.

CONTENTS

11 PREFACE *Alan Light*

13 FOREWORD *Quincy Jones*

15 INTRODUCTION *Danyel Smith*

21 THIS THUG'S LIFE *Kevin Powell*

33 WHO'S GONNA TAKE THE WEIGHT? *Alan Light*

37 *THUG LIFE, VOLUME 1* review *Cheo Hodari Coker*

39 HOW THE WEST WAS WON *Cheo Hodari Coker*

41 SWEATIN' BULLETS *Cory Johnson*

43 2PACALYPSE NOW *Kevin Powell*

45 READY TO LIVE *Kevin Powell*

53 *ME AGAINST THE WORLD* review *Danyel Smith*

63 ME (AND HER) AGAINST THE WORLD *Josh Tyrangiel*

65 HIT MAN *Allison Samuels*

67 FIGHT THE POWER *Joan Morgan*

71 LIVE FROM DEATH ROW *Kevin Powell*

79 ALL EYEZ ON HIM *Kevin Powell*

87 BULLETS OVER BROOKLYN

91 RUNNIN' MATES *David Bry*

93 FAITH. FULLY. *Karen R. Good*

94 STRAIGHT OFFA DEATH ROW *Joseph V. Tirella*

97 INSIDE THE MIND OF SHAKUR *VIBEonline*

103 WEST COAST IN THE HOUSE *OJ Lima*

105 STAYING POWER *Danyel Smith*

106 STAKES IS HIGH *The Blackspot*

113 FREAKY DEAKY *Chairman Mao*

115 IN THE EVENT OF MY DEMISE *Tupac Shakur*

116 READY TO DIE *Rob Marriott*

124 LAST TESTAMENT *Rob Marriott*

127 TO MY SON *Mutulu Shakur*

129 HOME AT LAST *Danyel Smith*

130 ALL THAT GLITTERS *Rob Marriott*

137 GOOD KNIGHT?

141 WELCOME TO THE TERROR ZONE *Sanyika Shakur*

144 SHOOK ONE *Sanyika Shakur*

147 STRICTLY FOR MY CLAZZMATEZ *Billy Jam*

149 *R U STILL DOWN? (REMEMBER ME)* review *Gabriel Alvarez*

150 HOLLER IF YA SEE ME *dream hampton*

152 AFTERWORDS: *John Singleton, Chuck D, Ernest Dickerson*

154 TIMELINE: LIVED FAST, DIED YOUNG

156 DISCOGRAPHY

157 FILMOGRAPHY

158 CONTRIBUTORS

159 CREDITS

PREFACE

This is VIBE's first venture into book publishing, and the subject could not be more appropriate. There is no other artist we have covered as extensively as Tupac Shakur—he has appeared on our cover four times in this young magazine's life span. But the reason was never, as Mobb Deep suggested in one single, that "VIBE magazine on some love shit." No other individual touched our readers like Tupac. There was no one else we consistently received so many letters about—some supporting him, some attacking him; but all full of such intense passion and feeling, so much love, so much anger.

The overwhelming response made it clear that Tupac had come to embody all the contradictions and confusion that have grown up around hip hop. He was a lightning rod, a screen onto which millions of people projected their feelings about rap, about race, and about the young black man in America today. Tupac may be a legend now, but he's hardly a hero. Many young people may have looked up to him, but he himself often seemed to be searching for a leader.

"Laugh Now, Cry Later" was tattooed on Tupac's back, but there is no later, no time for crying when you're dead at 25, and not much time to laugh, either. The real story behind his murder may or may not ever emerge, but nothing will change the end result: One more young black man is dead for no good reason, one more young life is ended long before its time. And it is incumbent on all of us in and around the hip hop community to remember that this death is no triumphant, blaze-of-glory exit but just another senseless murder. We need to do everything in our power to help stop the killing.

When I spoke to a longtime family friend of the Shakurs the day after his death, she said, "I know he's in heaven, I just hope he's not giving the angels too hard a time." Our thoughts are with Tupac's family and the fans who identified with him so strongly.

May Tupac Shakur rest in peace, and may the rest of us live in it.

Alan Light
Editor-in-Chief, VIBE *magazine*

INTRODUCTION *By Danyel Smith*

Tupac Shakur: a fiery ferocious MC, an auspicious actor, a man so beautiful he made you wanna touch the screen, the photograph, him. He made you wanna see those vanilla teeth, the wet sweet wild eyes, the fleshy lips, the lashes like fans like feathers on his fudgy skin. He made you want to kill him, defend him, make him your baby. He dared you to find the lies, to prove he's crazy. Tupac keeps you searching, even now, for the line between him and the him he put out there for you to see, for the line between being and acting, between how one rolls through life and how one rocks the microphone. Crazy motherfucker. Coward. Sucker. Sexist. Sex symbol. Superman. Provocateur. Hero.

He's another hero we don't need, and 'Pac's built, in death even, to last. From the start, his life was made-for-mythologizing, shrouded as it was in the tragedy of the Black Panther party. Because of his mother's affiliation with the group, Tupac's early existence was mingled with the plain logic of breakfast for everyone, in the ballsy resolve of guns in California's state capital, in the glamour and fraternity of leather pea-coats and tams for any brother wanting to stand up and fight—or look ferocious and fab. And Tupac's adult biography has everything—money, music, movies, malfeasance—that makes us love and hate someone. No matter what wrong shit he was ever caught up in, he always had his other raised-by-Panthers/fuck-tha-police self to fall back on.

Tupac's five albums are equal parts striking and adequate. His dramatic (on-screen) performances were promising here and cartoony there. He never quite lived up to the brilliance of his Bishop in Ernest Dickerson's 1992 *Juice*. Onstage, his performances were spotty. Tupac, like many MCs, rode his own dick, seeming to care more about how he was coming off to his boys backstage than he did about the average Negro who paid to stand up in a hot club and catch 'Pac's fever for a moment.

Tupac's different lives were very much in league, though; none would have been vibrant without the others. He managed them, like he managed his blackness—with a fantastic, desperate dexterity. Like most American heroes, Tupac Shakur had glide in his stride, big guns, and leather holsters. But his life was about juggling plums while bullets nipped at his ankles. It was about defiance, women, paranoia, ego, and anger—and going out in a blaze of what he imagined to be glory.

In the late 1980s and early 1990s, Tupac Shakur was chiseling out an existence in Marin City, California's craggy slums. Oakland was known as Coke-Land back then, and though it was a bridge or two away from Marin, Tupac got over to the East Bay a lot, first hanging with his half brother Mocedes and a crew known as Strictly Dope, then with this white girl, Leila Steinberg, from Sonoma County, who was managing him, and then with the droll brothers who made up Digital Underground.

To what degree it is true will probably go forever untold, but the rise of the Bay Area dope game and Bay Area hip hop were massively intertwined. (Actual gangsters, their stacks of cash, and the music business have been linked since kids in the 1940s gave music a real economy.) It's no coincidence that as the crack cocaine market exploded, people like DU, Too Short, and MC Hammer blew up—as well as lesser-known talents like MC Ant, Ant Banks, K-Cloud & the Crew, Premo, and Capitol Tax. The Oakland Police Department Drug Task Force was using battering rams to bust down the doors of dope houses back then. Kids were getting a gross kind of paid while Highland Hospital yanked bullets from bodies. There seemed a ceaseless stream of mothers, groggy with grief, wailing on the news about a good child who was dead. MCs and songwriters responded to the havoc crack was wreaking on the East Bay.

Hammer's contribution was the innocuous "Pray," but Tony Toni Toné went to the soul of the matter with 1988's "Little Walter," an ode to a dope dealer who gets shot upon opening his front door. Club Nouveau's 1986 "Situation #9" (a Top 10 R&B hit) was another admonition: "The life that you're living / Is gonna catch up to you / And boy, I think you need some help." The immense vocals balanced the paranoid lyrics, and that chemistry may have inspired Tupac to ask Roniece Livias to sing in the background (along with David Hollister, who would go on to sing lead in the first incarnation of Teddy Riley's BLACKstreet) of his debut single, 1991's "Brenda's Got a Baby."

Tupac's "Brenda" deserts her newborn, sells dope, then sex, and ends up (in the video for the song) the silent star of a crime scene. He came to kick it with the DU crew one night on a plush Sausalito houseboat Jimi "Chopmaster J" Dright had rented while recording an album under the name Force One Network for Qwest Records. The bay rocked us softly while we listened to "Brenda's Got a Baby" three or four times. Tupac held on to a frayed piece of ruled paper with the lyrics.

"No, she ain't somebody I know," he answered somebody's question. Tupac curled himself forward and laughed. "Y'all some simple muthafuckas," he said. "She's one a them girls we all know." He was 20, I think. The verse he rapped on DU's 1991 "Same Song" had been like a single french fry for a growing boy: "Now I clown around / When I hang around / With the Underground." Tupac felt he had more to say. His then-manager, Atron Gregory, was unable to convince Tommy Boy's Monica Lynch of Tupac's potential, but Interscope saw dollar signs in Tupac's worldview, and put up the dough so Tupac could have his say.

It all came out of him in *2Pacalypse Now* (1991), the words of a boy weary of doing the "Humpty Dance," and tired of standing on the corner in Marin City, selling weed. All the best songs on that album—"Young Black Male," "Rebel of the Underground," and the unwavering "Trapped," with Shock in the back murmuring "Nah / You can't keep the black man down"—are rank with the funk of a young man cooped up too long in somebody else's concept. *2Pacalypse* didn't sound like a DU spin-off because while the Underground Railroad production squad stuck with the liq-

uid bassiness that had succeeded for Digital, they also went for a sound more incensed, impassioned, broken, and hateful. They added some Tupac.

Tupac's MC skills were just coming together back then. His words, especially in "Brenda," are over-enunciated and urgent. His writing, though, was clear and picturesque. Brenda was "in love with a molester / Who's sexing her crazy." And when Tupac says "Prostitute found slain / And Brenda's her name / She's got a baby," with Hollister and Roniece battling out in the background, moaning and repeating the name Brenda over and over, the song is bold and melancholy—a crystalline morality tale. The line "She didn't know what to throw away / And what to keep," especially in the way Tupac hurls it out, consonants sharp and hard, says more about a young woman's angry bewilderment with life than some of the most adored female MCs ever have.

It was right before the release of *2Pacalypse Now* that Tupac, while in New York with Digital Underground, went to an audition with Ronald "Money-B" Brooks. Mun read before Ernest Dickerson, but didn't get called back. Tupac, who said he went

TUPAC KEEPS YOU SEARCHING, EVEN NOW, FOR THE LINE BETWEEN HIM AND THE HIM HE PUT OUT THERE FOR YOU TO SEE.

along "just to trip," ended up being cast opposite costar Omar Epps's tormented Q as Bishop in *Juice*. While the training Tupac received during his high-school years at Baltimore's School for the Arts no doubt emerged at the unscheduled audition, the way he hustled himself into the reading demonstrated a kind of alertness to opportunity that can't be taught in the classroom.

In the film, Tupac and Epps battle it out for most lovely—both of them black as truth with brown eyes, matching each other stare for stare. Q wants "juice," but the kind Bishop gets drunk on is too corrosive. Bishop has killed Raheem, one of his best friends, and at the funeral, his easy duplicity is marrow-freezing. And later, when Q, trying to get his life back together, slams his locker shut only to find Bishop standing there, it's a vision of one hellborn. The movie house gasps were loud and in unison. "It's over," says Bishop. "Ain't nothin' nobody can do about it now." And like so many of the words that came out of Tupac's mouth which seemed to predict his end, they provide a peek into his state of mind. "You know what?" he says. "I am crazy."

Tupac played Bishop-as-bogeyman ingeniously. Dickerson placed him throughout *Juice* as a cloaked figure—at one point

Bishop's red hood is pulled over his head, his face turned away from the camera, a fiend more likely to battle the X-Men than three of his buddies in Harlem. Tupac depicts Bishop's coldness as a hopelessness he finally submits to, even if it means embracing depravity. "You gotta get the ground beneath your feet, get the wind behind your back," says Bishop, after watching James Cagney get shot in *Public Enemy*. "And go out in a blaze of glory if you got to. Otherwise you might as well be dead your damn self." At the end of the film, to the strains of Cypress Hill's "How I Could Just Kill a Man," Q can't hold on to Bishop any longer. Bishop is hanging off the side of a building, Q holding on while he can. "Hold on, Bishop!" Q manages to say, then Bishop is gone—with us calling after him.

In 1991, Public Enemy was still the best band hip hop ever birthed. Touring with Anthrax, they came to the Calvin Simmons Auditorium in Oakland on October 20, the day that the Oakland Hills were burning down to the dirt. Smoke hung over the whole city, ashes fell to the ground like tiny gray snowflakes. Authorities were asking citizens to stay off the roads. Would the PE concert go on? Would Digital Underground roll to the show even though the condominium complex that housed three of the group's members was now among the ashes falling from the sky?

The mood backstage was bleak. This was only a few weeks before *Juice* came out, and somebody'd told me earlier in the day that Tupac had gotten in trouble with the police the day before, had gotten his ass beat in the middle of Oakland's tiny downtown. I saw him backstage, from across a long room, and he looked great. He was talking to someone; I could see his profile, and I knew that the story must have been exaggerated. I walked over to tell him what I'd heard and that he looked fine, and when I got up on him and his whole face was in my face I saw that the other side was puffed and scabby, his eye was swollen, there were scratches and small dents on his forehead—but just on the one side.

He laughed when he saw the expression on my face and gave me back his profile. "You like that better?" he said, with his usual toothy smile. "Nope!" he said, showing me his whole face again. "You gotta look! Look! Those motherfuckers had me on the ground and they bashed my head into the sidewalk over and over. On some bullshit! Hear me? Mad 'cause I had a check for seven grand in my wallet. I'ma sue 'em, though. Watch me." And he just kept on like that, talking to everybody, real regular, no bandages. One side of him flawless, the other ruined as the hills in flames behind us.

"Holler If Ya Hear Me," produced by Randy "Stretch" Walker of Live Squad, is the best track (and it was never a single) Tupac Shakur ever recorded. It's the first number on 1993's *Strictly 4 My N.I.G.G.A.Z.*, and it barrels at you, churning and fired up. "'Cause I'm black born / I'm supposed to say 'peace' / Sing songs / And get capped on?" The lines are juicy with testosterone, every one rolling right into the next. "Pump! Pump! if you're pissed / At the sellouts living it up / One way or another / They'll be giv-

ing it up." He's going fast with the lyrics, the song revved up on the intoxicating, pretend energy that comes from saying what you want when you know it's only about itself, not about what really happens, or about what you're really going to do. But still, it feels divine.

"Oh, no / I won't turn the other cheek." And it's like, yes. Can we not turn the other fucking cheek? Can we revel at the blood heating up our hearts when we hear a black person espousing that? "I love it when they fear me," says 'Pac, and how lovely is that feeling when you have always been in fear? Tupac emits fat zaps of musical electricity—they first rouse, then dull, then burn.

Tupac, with "Holler," dispensed a buccaneer spirit—bandanna'd men, fancy women, romance, mutiny. It's what gangsta rap was about at its N.W.A. beginnings: no more Mr. Nice Guy. Let's be defiant in our songs and we'll feel, if not actually be, free. We'll feel a part of the patriarchal club—every line of a good gangsta rap song being a warm hand on a soft dick, after all. And as usual, too-passive girls get the (sensual) benefit and pay the (political and spiritual) cost. Surrounded by rock nostalgia, hip hop fans believe that music "changed the world" before, so it can change the world again. Every time someone new arrives—Chuck D, Ice-T, Arrested Development's Speech, anyone from the Wu-Tang Clan—and dares to state what he (and it's always a he) thinks about the world, blacks get hopeful, whites get excited, and then when things stay the same, everyone feels betrayed.

It was around this time he was arrested for shooting two off-duty cops on October 31, 1993, in Atlanta. Shooting cops? And living to tell the story? And beating the rap? He was beyond real. He rhymed about shooting people, and getting shot, and he lived it in real life, and he played it on film. He filled the hero spot in a way someone like Eazy-E never could, because Eazy wasn't easy to look at and Eazy never talked about his mama or any other female like he loved her.

"Keep Ya Head Up" was the gold single that carried *Strictly* to platinum status. The song contains a riff from the Five Stairsteps' "O-o-h Child," and vocals from the same Dave Hollister (credited this time as the "Black Angel") who contributed so mightily to "Brenda's Got a Baby." On each of Tupac's albums, he included at least one song that illuminated the side of himself that believed in good. "I wanna give a holler to my sisters on welfare," he says in "Head Up." "Tupac cares if don't nobody else care." Uplifting, pro-choice, and anti-abuse, "Keep Ya Head Up," "Dear Mama," and "Brenda" are the "good" songs, the ones that make Tupac unassailable in the eyes of his fans. "Head Up," especially, is used like shield and sword to defend him.

Tupac tells women he knows they're "Dying inside / But outside you're looking fierce." It's a little saccharine at points, yes, but as "Head Up"'s chart success proved, by this time, Tupac Shakur could say "Keep hope alive" over a decent loop and sell mega units. Tupac was smart enough to risk feeling and appearing "positive." (The song gave someone like Nas, for instance, nerve enough to do a song like "If I Ruled the World [Imagine That]" in 1996.) As author Reverend Michael Eric Dyson might put it, Tupac Shakur knew to give us a little God with our gangsta rap.

Tupac was at his best on *Strictly 4 My N.I.G.G.A.Z.*, still touched by Digital Underground's mischeivous aura but standing on his own two feet, not yet doing time on Death Row. On "Representin' 93," Tupac names the brothers he loves–and in 1993, he was still referring to DU as his "real niggaz." "I Get Around" was pretty much a Digital Underground song with Tupac on lead. Listen and you can almost hear Shock-G in the studio telling 'Pac to lighten up a little bit–take a swim, have some sex, go platinum, live a little. Tupac was on his way to being deified or dead or both, is what everyone said. We watched him in his black Versace, knowing exactly which was correct.

In 1993's *Poetic Justice* Tupac is bald, extra slew-footed, and wears a huge nose ring. He looks pretty, but it doesn't matter because Regina King steals the movie from him, Janet Jackson, and Joe Torry. Much was made of Tupac playing a Regular Guy, not someone like Bishop, who was closer to what people believed to be Tupac's "real" personality, and therefore easy to play. He succeeded to a large degree, considering John Singleton's banal story line. What hurt the film most was the coldness between Shakur and Jackson. She'd requested he take an HIV test before she would even kiss him, and the sizzle, if there had been any, was imperceptible on the screen. In truth, Tupac wasn't easy around girls in his films or in his videos. There was bravado and awkwardness, but little smoothness.

TUPAC WAS ON HIS WAY TO BEING DEIFIED OR DEAD OR BOTH.

Because of creative differences and attitude contradictions, Tupac got booted from Allen and Albert Hughes's *Menace II Society* and then Singleton's *Higher Learning*. Burning bridges all over Hollywood's colored section, Tupac ended up in *Above the Rim* (1994), playing a murderous gangsta basketball scout. In the film, Tupac's bandannas coordinate with his every outfit, neatly folded and painstakingly pressed. He's like Doris Day at the beginning of 1959's *Pillow Talk*, perfectly dressed and bonneted and ready to rumble.

Tupac's character, Birdie, was flimsily written, but Tupac fully dramatized the deadness of soul certain killers must have. As in *Juice*, there are moments in *Rim* when Tupac captures the calm of bitter people who've been kicked when they were defenseless, the confidence that comes with constantly intimidating people. He does casual evil as deftly as John Malkovich, tells you all about Hades with his fringed eyes.

Above the Rim has its happy ending (Duane Martin's character goes to Georgetown on a basketball scholarship) but there's also Birdie's violent comeuppance. Marlon Wayans's character, Bugaloo, at the end of the film, raises a pistol to shoot Birdie. Tupac's mouth turns down in a sneer as the bullet hits him. He's pushed back, and his arms fly up over his head. In slow motion, Birdie looks like a spirit has entered him, or like he's pouring himself, in spurts, into some lover.

The spring Tupac was incarcerated–acquitted of sodomy and weapons charges, guilty of sexual abuse–his third album, *Me Against the World* (1995) was released, and debuted at number one on *Billboard*'s pop and R&B album charts. "Dear Mama," about Tupac's troubled but loving relationship with his mother, proved a perfect antidote to the charges. Particularly in a moment when some were beginning to wonder, If he didn't rape that girl in the hotel, why didn't he help her? Did he really nap through a gangbang? Why didn't he denounce his buddies like the guy who wonders, in "Keep Ya Head Up," "Why we take from our women / Why we rape our women / Why we hate our women"?

"Dear Mama," along with Tupac's appearance in court, bandaged and weak from the five bullets he took in the lobby of a New York City recording studio, smoothed his rough edges and filled in his story. And he didn't spend much time in jail, either. Tupac Shakur was rescued, like a true innocent, from New York's Clinton Correctional Facility.

Death Row Records CEO Suge Knight secured a bond for $1.4 million so Tupac could jet to southern California and begin recording what became the twenty-seven-song album *All Eyez on Me*. Tupac was entrenched in the Death Row camp by 1994, his production strictly L.A.-style. Tupac told me he couldn't deal with Atron Gregory "apologizing for him," and by 1995, Tupac was being managed by Suge himself, and had gone from being signed to Jimmy Iovine's Interscope to being signed to its subsidiary, Knight's Death Row Records.

Hip hop's first double album, *All Eyez on Me* went on to sell seven million units. Death Row cofounder and house producer Dr. Dre and Suge Knight were starting to fall out by the time Tupac began recording, and Dre produced only two tracks for *All Eyez*, one of them being the huge hit "California Love." Dre and Tupac trade verses, and Zapp's Roger Troutman, with his jheri curl and electronic voicebox still intact, makes the chorus unforgettable.

The rest of the album is mostly, to use one of Tupac's favorite words, simple. On "All About U," 'Pac, Snoop Doggy Dogg, Nate Dogg, and Dru Down chime in over a tinny sample of Cameo's "Candy." All of them, Tupac included, spit out labels for women–shitty-ass ho', hoochie–and one of them (doesn't matter who) says, "Is you sick from the dick / Or is it the flu?" Great sexist songs like Raekwon's "Ice Cream," DJ Quik's "Sweet Black Pussy," and even Too Short's grotesque "Freaky Tales" have either silliness or genuineness or art at their core. They seduce with inspired beats and intriguing chauvinisms. Many of the ditties on *All Eyez* are repulsive not only because the production is tired, but because the misogynist themes are weak, and break under the pressure of two or three listens. You can't even respect them for their intensity, let alone be offended or scared.

And it's not like everything has to be about peer marriages or keeping your head up. Tupac is at his most alluring on *All Eyez*'s "How Do U Want It?" Words like "Tell me / Is it cool to fuck?" tumble from his mouth like dice. "Holla at Me" packs none of the same punch as "Holler If Ya Hear Me," but the last two songs on *All Eyez on Me* reflect 'Pac's fight-and-fuck, love-and-hate, boast-and-beg dichotomies. "Ain't Hard 2 Find" is 'Pac, E-40, B-Legit, C-Bo, and Richie Rich acting like he-men. If you wanna fight, I'm right here, is what these California soul brothers are saying. "Heaven Ain't Hard 2 Find," on the other hand, is Tupac at his macho sweetest, creating a scene complete with Alizé and "moonlight mist."

"We'll be best friends," he almost sings to his intended, "I'll be the thug in your life." Tupac sympathizes with his lover's hesitancy (if she wasn't hesitant, she'd be a hoochie in another song). Then he says "Love me for my thug nature," sounding foolish at first, but then desolate, and in the end, profoundly sad.

In *Bullet*, it's Mickey Rourke, as a bandanna'd white *cholo*, who's constantly getting in touch with his thug nature. The film opens with Rourke riding away from prison in a blue convertible with Barry White playing in the background. Tupac sports an eye patch, and rides around in the back of a limo slicing a mango with a switchblade, looking like somebody snatched him off the set of one of his own video shoots. Watching *Bullet* is like getting teeth pulled without Novocain while listening to the post–Lionel Richie Commodores. Tupac and Rourke look loaded most of the time (even when there's no need for them to) and reek of a desperation totally detached from their characters.

Bullet never made it to the cineplexes, and is easily forgotten in the face of *Gridlock'd*, a flat, goofy, good film Tupac starred in with Tim Roth, which was released six months after Tupac's death. When Tupac, as the heroin-addicted Spoon, says "Somehow I don't think this was my mother's dream for me," squinting as the drug dances through his blood, "Dear Mama" suddenly sounds less like an image Band-Aid. Spoon is a bass player/poet on the spoken word scene, and at the end, when he's kicked, and he raps a corny rhyme about life being like a traffic jam, he carries it off, but you can't imagine Tupac ever recording anything like that in real life, ever. The songs he recorded right before he was shot dead in Las Vegas bear no resemblance to anything in *Gridlock'd*.

The Don Killuminati: The 7 Day Theory (1996) is dreary because Tupac was no longer here when it came out, and powerful only in the quickest and most tragic ways. Tupac—rather, "Makaveli" as an ominous voice states—says in "Bomb First" that he's got "Thug Life running through my veins on strong." Then he chants, and it's pitiful, "West coast ridah / Comin' up behind ya / Shoulda neva fucked wit' me." No? Well, they did, and now you're dead. But dead or not, the mighty "Hail Mary" is one of Tupac's better songs (though in an attempt to sound ominous, Tupac sounds

much like Shaquille O'Neal on the mike). "Come wit' me / (Hail Mary, nigga) / Run quick see . . . Do you wanna ride or die?" "White Man'z World" is 'Pac's usual shout-out to the sisters. In "Against All Odds," Tupac disrespects Mobb Deep, Nas, and Sean "Puffy" Combs, like he did so fervently in "Hit 'Em Up," a base diatribe/revenge fantasy Death Row released in June 1996. "I knew you niggas from way back," he says in "Odds" when he's not spitting out more spiteful disses about their personal skills ("Nas / Your shit is bitten"). In the song, Tupac is consumed with other people wanting and stealing his style, his life, his way of being.

Tupac, especially on his first two albums, considered himself blameless, made it clear, especially before he got down with Death Row and the whole L.A. ridah scene, that his life was not his fault. In *Strictly 4 My N.I.G.G.A.Z*'s "Strugglin'" he says "Some call me crazy / But this is what you gave me." In that same album's "Pac's Theme (Interlude)," Tupac answers a pseudo-reporter's question, "I was raised in this society / So there's no way you can expect me to be a perfect person / I'ma do what I'ma do." He always did believe, or at least believed strongly when I knew him, that to be crazy in this world was to be normal, that to get along well in a place so inherently unfair was to have eaten yourself alive and then be living on the shit that you pushed out afterward.

Tupac made people uncomfortable. At his best, he called blacks and whites alike out on their complicity in a despicable system. He made thuggery-as-resistance appealing, urged us to be loud and wild and reckless. He was not trying to "rise above" the way things are. He was not trying to "be better." No one ever said what would happen if folks got tired of aspiring to dignity; Tupac showed one way it already is. "I love it when they fear me," he said. But more truly, he loved not fearing them. He was free when he didn't give a fuck about anything, including continuing his own life, when he felt like the world—for a change—was his.

Wasn't Tupac great when he wasn't getting shot up? Or accused of rape? Wasn't he just the best when he wasn't falling for Suge Knight's lame-ass lines and dying broke? Couldn't Tupac just have been your everything? He got you fired up, excited and hopeful about something you couldn't even name, then had you crying in the end for a smooth-skinned young man in a coffin, like always. But you wish him back for one more song, one more standoff with the cops, more jail time, more anything. You wish back the bright spectacle that was Tupac Amaru Shakur's noisy sad life. Short life. Thug life. Triple life. Afterlife.

The last sound on *The Don Killuminati* is that of bullets popping off. Helicopter blades beat the air into a small, inside-out tornado. Tupac is dead in the street. Blood everywhere. Police clearing the scene. Thug niggas stand on the periphery, girls cry. Commentators report the shooting of "Tupack Shaker." He's dead, they say, dancing from star to star at night, diving into Hell's seething sewers at dawn. Tupac bathes on Sundays in the tears we cry for him, wades like a slave through that troubled water.

THIS THUG'S LIFE

With assault and sodomy charges pending from coast to coast, Tupac Shakur appears to be a rising star out of control. Is Tupac a menace to society or just to himself?
By Kevin Powell

i see you blackboy
bent toward destruction watching
for death with tight eyes
—Sonia Sanchez, poet

It's a brisk Wednesday morning in November—the day before Thanksgiving—and courtroom 120 at 100 Centre Street in downtown Manhattan is filled to capacity with mostly black and Latino men. There is a uniform sense of disillusionment among them: Some slump on the long benches while others reflexively spin their bodies around every so often to see who is coming into court. There would be little excitement on this day were it not for the presence of the media and a celebrity defendant. "That's Tupac!" a gap-toothed black girl whispers with glee to no one in particular. Two broad-chested white boys with thick Queens accents join in the chorus of saying his name as if they, too, had made a great discovery.

Tupac Shakur notices none of this and glances from time to time at today's presiding judge. Charged with sodomy and sexual abuse, Tupac has been at the center of a heavy media barrage for the past week, made more intense by the arrests of two other hip hop icons, Snoop Doggy Dogg and Flavor Flav. The New York City papers have reported that on November 18, Tupac allegedly forced himself on a black 20-year-old woman he had met days before at a local club. The woman claims that she went to visit Tupac at the Parker Meridien, a posh Manhattan hotel, and that they embraced in his bedroom. When, moments later, three of Tupac's friends came in, she tried to leave. But, she charges, the four men held her there, pulled her hair, sexually abused her, and sodomized her numerous times. As the prosecutor put it, Tupac "liked her so much, he decided to share her as a reward for his boys." These charges come only a few weeks after Tupac was arrested in Atlanta for allegedly shooting two off-duty police officers and released on $55,000 bail.

In an effort to rebut the charges and beat back the negative publicity, Tupac's attorney, Michael Warren, has charged law-enforcement officials in New York with erasing sexually explicit telephone messages to Tupac left by the accuser. Warren claims that on November 14—the night Tupac and his accuser met—eyewitnesses saw the young woman engaging in oral sex with the rapper on the dance floor of the club. Further, the prosecutor has admitted the woman testified to having had consensual sex with him that night. In a press conference scheduled for later this week, Warren plans to introduce Michelle Fuentes, an 18-year-old fan who visited him at his hotel without incident, in the hopes of portraying Tupac's relationships with women as amiable. The lawyer says his team has interviewed a number of young women who've had encounters—sexual or otherwise—with Tupac and that, "as time goes on, you'll see more young ladies step forward" as character witnesses.

But Tupac's taste for posing with guns and publicly dissin' black women (one young black woman has claimed Tupac berated her in the hotel lobby at last year's Black Radio Exclusive convention) make one wonder how he can survive any of this. That these charges coincide with his biggest hit ever, the Top 10 "Keep Ya Head Up"—which both praises women and criticizes men for disrespecting them—is emblematic of Tupac's contradictory nature.

With a cloud of controversy surrounding him and a movie in progress—he has been in New York City shooting the high school basketball drama *Above the Rim,* directed by Jeffrey Pollack—Tupac looks nothing like the happy-go-lucky 22-year-old I met at the black-music convention "Jack The Rapper" in Atlanta last August. Back then the surprisingly tall Tupac was fresh off his starring role in *Poetic Justice* opposite Janet Jackson, and his single "I Get Around" was jacking the rap charts. Unsure what to make of him as he stood in the hotel lobby absorbing the "oohs" and "ahhs" of female and male admirers alike, I introduced myself. The posing stopped—at least momentarily—and Tupac gave me a pound and exclaimed loudly, "Whassup, nigga?! You my man from that MTV show. I had your back, dog. . . ."

Today, Tupac is just a shadow of that B-boy machismo. Surrounded by an entourage of black men of various hues and sizes, he steps before the judge with his codefendants, looking like a lost little boy. The charges are read, he is given a return date, and the reporters ready themselves outside the courthouse. On the night of his arrest, Tupac puffed up his chest and cold-smacked the media: "I'm young, black . . . I'm making money and they can't stop me. They can't find a way to make me dirty, and I'm clean." But as he and his entourage move out of the courtroom today, that defiance is tucked away, enveloped by the muscular arms of security guards who push him through the throng, into a waiting van that speeds off, leaving news teams on the curb befuddled.

Before all this trouble, before the New York and Atlanta cases, no one was eager to tell the story of Tupac Shakur, save a few fanzines. As his career evolved and as his brushes with the law piled up, I kept mental notes, preparing for interviews that would eventually provide the basis for a piece not just about a rapper but about the young-black-male identity crisis in America today, about the troubling contradictions inherent in hip hop culture, 1994. Tupac seemed a fitting symbol, a lightning rod, in fact, for many of these issues.

But then the story changed. Yeah, he *is* an angry young black man. But why is he so angry? Where did he come from? What compels him to say and do the things that he does? Are the cases pending against Tupac Shakur merely coincidences, part of an elaborate "setup," as his lawyers would have us believe, or evidence of a deeper problem? Is he the symbolic young black man shackled by the system, or an individual young black man out of control?

Tupac seemed on the verge of a breakdown as I pursued this interview in November and December, calling his publicist, his manager, his record company, close friends, even his mother. The media had been unfair, they said, and he didn't want to talk anymore. He finally agreed to talk to me, perhaps because I had been working on the story long before these arrests, and perhaps because he saw it as his one good chance to tell his side of the story.

T upac has always been the person who's made up the game—always," says Afeni Shakur, Tupac's 47-year-old mother, a week after his New York arraignment and a day after a hearing in Atlanta. A tiny, dark-complexioned woman with close-cropped hair

and deeply etched dimples, Afeni lives in a modest apartment in Decatur, Georgia, an Atlanta suburb, and speaks with an urgency that, she says, comes from her lifelong political activism. "He would have make-believe singing groups," she continues, "and he would be Prince, or Ralph in New Edition. He was always the lead."

But life wasn't quite that simple for Tupac Amaru Shakur. Named after an Inca chief, *Tupac Amaru* means "shining serpent," referring to wisdom and courage. *Shakur* is Arabic for "thankful to God." Although he was shaped by many of the problems of inner-city youths growing up in post–civil rights America—poverty, fatherlessness, constant relocation—Tupac's story began even before he was born.

Afeni Shakur (born Alice Faye Williams in North Carolina) was "like everyone else in the early '60s and watched the civil rights movement on television." A member of the notorious Disciples gang as a teenager, Afeni points to two primary factors that channeled her frustrations in a political direction: the historic Ocean Hill–Brownsville, Brooklyn, parent-student strike (where her nephew was a student) in 1968 and the formation of the Black Panther Party in New York City.

Founded in 1966 in Oakland by Huey P. Newton and Bobby Seale, the Panthers quickly grew into a radical wing of the civil rights movement, with support in the hardcore ghettos as well as white patronage from the likes of Jane Fonda and Leonard Bernstein. Best known for their militant display of guns and insurgent tactics, which earned them FBI surveillance and raids, the Panthers were also a community-based organization that provided free breakfast for children and free health clinics in black neighborhoods across the nation.

Afeni joined in September 1968. In April 1969 she and twenty other members of the New York Panthers were arrested and charged with numerous felonies, including conspiracy to bomb several public areas in New York City. The case dragged on for twenty-five months. While out on bail, Afeni courted two men—Legs, a straight-up gangster ("He sold drugs, he did whatever he needed to make money"), and Billy, a member of the Party. She had previously been married to Lumumba Shakur, one of her codefendants who remained incarcerated. When he found out she was pregnant, he divorced her.

When Afeni's bail was revoked in early 1971, she found herself at the Women's House of Detention in Greenwich Village, pregnant with Tupac. While defending herself in the Panther 21 case, she says she had to fight to receive "one egg and one glass of milk per day" for herself and her unborn son. Tears fill her eyes at the memory. "I never thought he'd make it here alive."

In May 1971, Afeni and thirteen of her colleagues were acquitted of all charges. A month later, on June 16, Tupac was born. Her hands shaking, Afeni leans forward, clasps her fingers around a cigarette, and inhales deeply. She touches her lips and thinks for a moment.

"I was scared they were gonna take my child when he was born," she says, her elbows pushing hard on her knees. "I was nuts and out of it. The doctor took the baby right to my sister, who was standing outside so that she could tell me later . . ." She begins to cry. "So that she could identify him later and tell me it was really my child."

M y mother was hella real with me," Tupac says later the same day, as he takes a long, reflective drag on a cigarette, sitting on a sofa in his new home outside Atlanta. "She just told me, 'I

Growing
up, I
could
cook,
clean,
and sew,
but I just
didn't
feel
hard.

When they told me my moms was buy

don't know who your daddy is.' It wasn't like she was a slut or nothin'. It was just some rough times."

Rough times meant Afeni juggling her political activities with the economic realities of raising two children. Tupac says his family moved between the Bronx and Harlem a lot, sometimes living in homeless shelters. "I remember crying all the time," he says. "My major thing growing up was I couldn't fit in. Because I was from everywhere, I didn't have no buddies that I grew up with.

"Every time I had to go to a new apartment, I had to reinvent myself. People think just because you born in the ghetto you gonna fit in. A little twist in your life and you don't fit in no matter what. If they push you out of the 'hood and the white people's world, that's criminal." He brushes smoke away with his hand. "Hell, I felt like my life could be destroyed at any moment . . ."

Tupac still wears a lot of gold—"old-school jewels," as he calls them—and his pants, baggy khakis, are still wrapped around the crack of his ass. With his razor-sharp cheekbones, long, feminine eyelashes that curve upward at the edges, and bushy eyebrows framing his distinctive, wide, and piercingly dark brown eyes, he looks like the black prince he says his mother's friends called him as a boy. And this split-level home is his castle. It has a 45-inch color television in the living room tuned to an all-music video channel, a basement where he plans to build a recording studio, and a huge backyard with a pool. Sneakers, packs of Newports, empty fast-food bags, and piles of CDs and audio and video cassettes cover the floors. Members of Thug Life, Tupac's posse, stroll in and out. This ghettocentric enclave is on a block where white folks, he says, are frightened of all the young black men driving Mercedeses and BMWs and playing their music real loud. In Tupac Shakur, I guess they think they have their worst nightmare as a neighbor.

"I was lonely," he says in a hushed tone. He played a lot of games as a kid to escape. "I didn't have no big brothers, no big cousins until later. I could remember writing songs, like real love songs. I remember writing poetry." A look of excitement crosses his face. "I remember I had a book like a diary. And in that book I said I was going to be famous." His mood swings again. "Looking back, I see that as the actor in me. Because I had that fucked-up childhood. The reason why I could get into acting was because it takes nothin' to get out of who I am to get into somebody else."

When Tupac was 12, Afeni enrolled him in the 127th Street Ensemble, a theater group in Harlem. "I wanted Tupac to focus on something since he was becoming of age," she says. In his first performance, Tupac played Travis in *A Raisin in the Sun*.

Tupac leans back on the sofa and beams at the memory. "Right now I can remember the bug biting me right there. I lay on a couch and played sleep for the first scene. Then I woke up and I was the only person onstage. I can remember thinking"—he lowers his voice to a whisper—"'This is the best shit in the world!' That got me real high. I was gettin' a secret: This is what my cousins don't do."

At the same time, though, he was having trouble squaring his mother's political views with his life. "She was trying to make me live this white picket fence lifestyle, but yet we ain't got no money and no food and no lights." Says Tupac: "You want me to go to school? They tellin' me all this stuff about the system but they pushin' us in the system. What type of shit is that?"

Perhaps more significantly, Tupac says he felt "unmanly" because he was fatherless. "All my cousins was like, 'You too pretty.' I didn't have hard features. I don't know, I just didn't feel hard," he says with exasperation. "I could cook, I could do clothes, I could sew, clean up the house. I could do all the things my mother could give me, but she couldn't give me nothing else."

Tupac admits these are the forces that drove him to the streets of New York. And to the life of Legs, the father he claimed. "I see him in me even now," he says. A classic city hustler once affiliated with legendary drug kingpin Nicky Barnes, Legs came to live with the family in the early 1980s and introduced Afeni to crack. "That was our way of socializing," she acknowledges. "He would come home late at night and stick a pipe in my mouth." Legs eventually wound up in prison—he had been arrested many times—for credit card fraud. By the time he was out, Afeni, tired of the hard times in New York, had moved her family to Baltimore. By the time Afeni called back to New York to let Legs know of her move, he had died from a crack-induced heart attack at 41.

"That hurt Tupac," she says, her eyes looking at her bare feet. "It fucked him up. It was three months before he cried. After he did, he told me, 'I miss my daddy.'"

"I was real bitter about Legs's death," Tupac says, "because I believe a mother can't give a son ways on how to be a man. Especially not a black man. It made me bitter seeing all these other niggas with fathers gettin' answers to questions that I have. Even now I still don't get 'em."

Baltimore was the first place Tupac began to feel an identity of his own. "I remember writing my first rap there. My name was MC New York. That's when I started fitting in. I was starting to get a name." He auditioned and was accepted by the Baltimore School for the Arts, where he finally felt in touch with himself. And with a different reality.

"The white kids had things we never seen. That was the first time I saw there was white people who you could get along with. Before that, I just believed what everybody else said: They was devils. But I loved it. I loved going to school. It taught me a lot. I was starting to feel like I really wanted to be an artist." He pauses, grins mischievously: "I was fucking white girls."

"I found him to be an extremely talented young actor," says Donald Hickens, head of the school's theater department. "He was confident and willing to take risks. He was very serious in the studio." Then Hickens—who is white—adds this: "For Tupac it was a new

ing dope, I, like, lost respect for her.

addiction, and now works for 2Pacalypse Entertainment, her son's management and production company. Meanwhile, Tupac compensated for her absence by "representing D.U. like a gang." He talks passionately of how he "gained points" on the road, "not taking shit from anyone. Everybody knew me even though my album wasn't out yet. I never went to bed. I was working it like a job. That was my number-one thing when I first got in the business. Everybody's gonna know me."

The first time I encountered Tupac Shakur, he scared a lot of people. It was in his role as Bishop in *Juice*. Directed by Spike Lee's cinematographer Ernest R. Dickerson, *Juice* was a mediocre attempt at capturing black-boy angst. But Tupac's dark, brooding performance as a juvenile delinquent-turned-psychopath outlasted the film and left us with the prophetic line: "I am crazy. But you know what else, I don't give a fuck!"

"He's what they call a natural," says John Singleton, the writer-director of *Boyz N the Hood* and *Poetic Justice*. "You know, he's a real actor. He has all these methods and everything, philosophies about how a role should be played."

The critical acclaim Tupac received for his role (the *New York Times* called him "the film's most magnetic figure") and the release of his debut album, *2Pacalypse Now,* signaled the beginning of a new phase in Tupac's life. "I loved the fact that I could go to any ghetto and be noticed and be known."

It also marked a new reason to exist: Thug Life.

On a balmy September day at the Marcus Garvey School in South Central Los Angeles, Tupac stands before a room full of teachers and administrators, mostly women, and explains Thug Life. "It's a double finger when you see people dressing like this," he says, pointing to his sagging jeans, pushing them down for extra emphasis. I scan the audience and everyone is listening intently. "Thug Life" is what Tupac calls his mission for the black community—a support group, a rap act, and a philosophy. Thug Life was given its acronym after the fact: The Hate U Gave Lil Infants Fuck Everybody.

"But why be a thug?" an elderly man asks.

"Because if I don't, I'll lose everything I have. Who else is going to love me but the thugs?"

I think of Tupac's music: It's a cross between Public Enemy and N.W.A., between Black Power ideology and "Fuck tha Police!" realism. When he raps, Tupac is part screaming, part preaching, part talking shit. The music is dense and, at times, so loud it drowns out the lyrics. You cannot dance to it. Perhaps that is intentional.

"Nobody can talk about pain like Tupac. No one knows it like me," he says. "It separates me from other rappers. All that pain I'm talking about in my rap, you can see it." All too clearly sometimes. Apparently, it is not just something he works out in his music or in his acting—it's something he carries into his relationships with women, with his peers, with authority figures. He seems incapable of separating art from life.

First, there was Oakland: In 1991, Tupac was arrested for jaywalking and resisting arrest, and has a $10 million claim against the police for alleged brutality. Then, in 1992, during a confrontation with old

acquaintances at a festival celebrating Marin City's fiftieth anniversary, a 6-year-old boy was shot in the head. No criminal charges have been filed against Tupac, but a civil suit is pending. Later that year, a Texas woman filed a multimillion-dollar civil suit against him, claiming that the young black man who killed her husband—a cop—had been influenced by Tupac's music.

Then there is 1992's *In Living Color* incident. Tupac had just arrived at the Fox lot to tape a segment when he claims his "limo driver disrespected my homeboy, screaming at him like he was less than a man. Then the limo driver went to his trunk. We didn't know if the guy was getting a gun or what." Tupac and his friend jumped out of the car and allegedly attacked the driver. Tupac was arrested but the charges have been dropped.

Finally, a year ago, Tupac got into a fight with directors Albert and Allen Hughes over the loss of his role in *Menace II Society.* The Hughes brothers will not comment on the case. Tupac, however, has a lot to say.

"They was doin' all my videos," he says. "After I did *Juice,* they said, 'Can we use your name to get this movie deal?' I said, 'Hell,

SINGLETON WANTED TUPAC TO BE "DE NIRO TO HIS SCORSESE," BUT HAD TO DROP HIM FROM HIS NEXT FILM.

yeah.' When I got with John Singleton, he told me he wanted to be 'Scorsese to your De Niro.' For starring roles I just want you to work with me. So I told the Hughes brothers I only wanted a little role. But I didn't tell them I wanted a sucker role. We was arguing about that in rehearsal. They said to me, 'Ever since you got with John Singleton's shit you changed.' They was trippin' 'cuz they got this thing with John Singleton. They feel like they competing with him."

The Hughes brothers dropped Tupac from *Menace* (Tupac says he found out watching MTV), and then, a few months later, ran into him at the taping of a Spice1 video. Tupac stepped to the twins ("That's a fair fight, am I right? Two niggas against me?"), hit Allen, and Albert ran off. Allen's civil suit against Tupac was still pending as VIBE went to press.

When I spoke with John Singleton in September about Tupac's problems, he said, "Everybody needs to fuckin' chill out and understand that this is a black man that's still tryin' to grow, you know?" By December, Singleton, who Tupac considers his "one friend in Hollywood" and was planning to cast the rapper as the lead in his next film, *Higher Learning,* was forced by Columbia Pictures to drop his star because of Tupac's recent arrests in Atlanta and New York. "Basically, since all this stuff is happening, the media is trying to play 'good nigga versus bad nigga' and say I don't want him in the movie," Singleton says. "That ain't true. In their minds, it doesn't matter if he's guilty or not. They don't want nothin' to do with him. I talked to Tupac and said, 'I still got your back.'"

Atlanta is considered the black mecca for the '90s. It is here that black folks can own businesses and homes, run city government, attend historically black colleges, create a thriving music industry à la L.A. Reid and Babyface, Dallas Austin, and Jermaine Dupri, and feel empowered. It is also here that Tupac's manager decided to purchase a home for his client, "so he can have a calmer life."

But on October 31, just a few days after moving in, Tupac was arrested for allegedly shooting two white off-duty police officers, brothers Mark and Scott Whitwell. The Whitwells were in the midst of a traffic-related argument when Tupac and his entourage pulled up. What happened next remains unclear. The Whitwells say Tupac fired at them; other witnesses say Mark Whitwell was the first to pull a gun. Tupac contends that he was merely coming to the aid of a black man the Whitwells were harassing. Charged with two counts of aggravated assault and released on bail, Tupac and his attorneys maintain he and his associates were acting in self-defense. On the day of Tupac's hearing, Mark Whitwell was charged with aggravated assault, and the investigating detective admitted the officers' report stated that "niggers came by and did a drive-by shooting."

The sexual-assault case in New York is more complicated. The details

WHO'S GONNA TAKE THE WEIGHT?

As this issue goes to press, two of hip hop's rising young stars—Snoop Doggy Dogg and Tupac Shakur—are awaiting trial for murder and aggravated assault. In a separate incident, Shakur has also been charged with sex abuse and sodomy. One of rap's most familiar names, Flavor Flav, was also arrested in a shooting incident. The national media is once again flaming with questions and accusations: "When Is Rap 2 Violent?" asks *Newsweek*'s cover, while *Time* adds, snidely, "[Snoop's] debut album is a hit. Possibly that murder charge helped?"

It's too easy to demonize the music, to hold it responsible for the violence in our cities, or to confuse these artists' lives with their work. It is equally foolish, though, to deny the possibility of any wrongdoing and dismiss the arrests as part of a racist conspiracy. Though these men are clearly troubled, they're innocent until proven guilty. But in the wake of these tragic events, we hardly need a trial to convict the hip hop industry—and by extension the music business as a whole: Guilty on all counts of exploiting and abandoning rappers, as it has done throughout the music's history. Guilty of looking at rappers as flavors of the month, to be discarded as soon as the next thing comes along. Guilty of marketing artists' "bad boy" images without concern for the consequences. Guilty of giving virtually no thought to decent management or career development—the safety net required for young, raw talent suddenly thrust into the spotlight.

The only other business in which 20-year-old inner-city kids receive million-dollar contracts and appear on magazine covers is sports. In sports, though, as soon as a young prospect starts to show real promise, scouts, agents, managers, and handlers come out like sharks. Maybe the athlete's best interest isn't always the first thing on their minds, but at least they provide a support system that a newcomer can lock into and lean on.

What is there for a hot new rapper? The pop music establishment still has no idea what to make of him, so they often leave the job of management to family members or friends from around the way. These folks may be likable and trustworthy, but with complicated, six-figure careers hanging in the balance, that's simply not enough.

Last month, a rapper may have been on the streets, in school or, yes, maybe in a gang (an image record labels are all to eager to promote). Overnight, he's on MTV, his pockets filled with cash, kids rolling up on him, saying, "Yeah? You think you're bad?" He's getting propositioned, hustled, sweated, all the while needing to prove that he hasn't lost touch with the streets. And then people act shocked when he winds up in trouble. Or they're not surprised at all, insisting that he's just a victim—one more black man that the System didn't want to see succeed.

Of course, our hip hop heroes must be held responsible for their own actions; inappropriate or illegal behavior cannot simply be pawned off on someone else. But the fact is that this music has now been around for a full generation and it's still treated like a fad by the industry. With multimillion-dollar profits must come responsibility. You can count on one hand the number of record companies that give real thought to planning these artists' careers, making hard decisions and determining long-term strategies. The number of hip hop managers who truly understand the music, the realities of business, and the unique demands of rappers and their audience is even smaller.

"Don't be satisfied with just selling a song," Chuck D once advised, "because we've been selling a lot of songs and dances." The emphasis should not be on rappers getting all the glory, he said, but on fans getting involved in all aspects of the business and "really kicking ass." The hip hop nation needs to be shown that skills on the mike aren't the only way to get large and take charge.

In 1971, Kool & the Gang posed the musical question "Who's Gonna Take the Weight?" Twenty years later, Gang Starr borrowed that title and asked again, this time addressing hip hop fans. We're still waiting for an answer. *Alan Light*

After reading about Tupac's past experiences with parental "loss" (his mother's addiction to drugs), his life of loneliness, and his quest to belong in places where people continually made him an outcast, I immediately asked, Will much of AmeriKKKa feel that this is an attempt on Tupac's part to gain sympathy and compassion in order to beat his bad "rap"? I hope not. This "fairy tale"—no matter how unreal it may seem to most—is the very real nightmare many of our young black men face every day.

Shawnda D. Hunt
Bronx, NY

APRIL 1994

Tupac's declaration of love and respect for black women causes me to question the depth of his understanding of the word "respect." His saying he allowed a "sister" to belittle him and herself by "going down" on him in public reflects the let-them-hoes-know mentality that is corrupting the minds and actions of our beautiful black children. Thousands of us have managed to survive those same ghettos of despair and still maintain our dignity, love, and respect for ourselves and the black community without the suburban-school breaks and financial

luxuries afforded Tupac. Offering no apologies for a slew of negativity toward women of color, Tupac has manipulated Kevin Powell in a feeble attempt to pimp his past as a weak justification of what I perceive as a big, bald head gone bad. Instead of dreaming a death of saving some white kid, I suggest that his time would be better spent living to save other misguided, miseducated, "misunderstood" black brothers like himself. Wake up, Tupac. This shit is a reality check!

Dana Malette Murray
Elizabeth, NJ

At some point Tupac has to start taking responsibility for his actions. He is aware of his past wrongdoings and recognizes them as such. But it seems like he is using his childhood—lacking a male influence to teach him how to "be a man," moving around a lot—as an excuse for his adult actions. These are not good excuses. He must grow up at some point. It seems he tried to "be a man" and develop an identity. It sounds like he was doing fine until he made the effort to become "hard." "Hard" is inner strength, not outer actions. "Hard" is being your own man, not trying to impress other men or women by putting on a front,

even if that entails cooking, sewing, and cleaning. Maybe now that he has chosen his "thug life" and has reached his interpretation of "hard," he's happy. But where has it gotten him—criminal charges, negative press, the opportunity to f——— any ho he chooses (black or white) whenever he wants? If that's hard, then I'm looking for a "soft" guy. If the rape and sodomy charges are proved true, my rap sheet on Tupac will list "hypocrite." It will show that everything he said on his pro-female anthem, "Keep Ya Head Up," was nothing but lies. I hate the thought of that. I hope Tupac's cleared of all charges and that he can continue his promising music and film careers as planned.

Kori J. Gerland
Houston, TX

I'm a 19-year-old college student, majoring in communications. When I read that Tupac said, "Growing up, I could cook, clean, and sew, but I just didn't feel hard," I said out loud, "That's what's wrong with the black males now: They think things like this are 'soft.' They need to stop making these movies and videos with gangs and guns and start showing more productive shit."

Tunisha Brown
Trenton, NJ

Tupac needs to take responsibility for his actions. He's using his childhood as an excuse for his adult actions.

Perhaps the most revealing thing about hip hop in 1994 is that the same "Mocedes the Mellow" who rhymed "a capello" on Tony Toni Toné's ecstatic 1990 single "Feels Good" is now a gangsta rapper. No one's accusing Mocedes, who is also Tupac Shakur's older brother, of faking the funk—his cameo on the Tonys' *The Revival* was a smart, career-boosting move. And with *Volume 1,* where he's joined by his notorious sibling and other guys down with the Thug Life groove-ment, Mocedes has made another shrewd move. Now he's MoPreme.

In an effort to capture the ear of both middle and urban America, MoPreme & Co. step up to the plate with dozens of metaphors for hardness. It's the same story you've heard on countless other records—"Mama-did-the-best-she-could-but-I'm-that-crazy-nigga." Or "I'm-fuckin'-hoes-and-smokin'-bitch-ass-marks-who-fail-to-recognize." The same P-Funk and Isley Brothers samples are there, the same funk crooning, and the same lyrics that look for solutions to black community problems at the bottom of a forty-ounce bottle.

Not to say that the formula isn't compelling when the groove hits the spot. The blues guitar licks on the first single, "Pour Out a Little Liquor," are the wind behind Tupac's lyrical sails—he kicks rhymes in a relaxed fashion, instead of spitting them like he usually does. But *Volume 1* shows only one side of the so-called gangsta psyche: getting paid and avenging for dead homies. There's little that reflects the futility of all the violence, or the daily stresses that lead countless kids down this path.

Volume 1 is mostly party-in-the-'hood music, an excuse for white teenagers in the Midwest to pull their caps down low and throw up fake gang sets because the songs give them a chance to assume the posture without feeling the pain—little wonder the introduction to "Str8 Balling" directly addresses this growing demographic. N.W.A's *Straights Outta Compton* (1988) came out as strong and progressive as Melvin Van Peebles's 1971 film *Sweet Sweetback's Baadasssss Song,* but Thug Life's *Volume 1* is more like *Hell Up in Harlem*: more style than content, more running than fighting, and a whole lot of shooting without thinking.

Cheo Hodari Coker

2PACALYPSE NOW

When the smoke clears from the trials, suits, allegations, and sentencings involving rapper/actor Tupac Shakur, his budding legend will have solidified in America's ghettos—and beyond. Shakur, the victim of an apparent stickup on November 30, resisted the gunmen, talking shit the whole time. He caught at least four bullets, underwent surgery, then left the hospital against doctors' orders less than twenty-four hours after being critically wounded. The next day, he was cleared of all but one charge in a highly publicized New York rape case. Back in October 1993, he allegedly shot at two Atlanta policemen, but the charges were dropped. Nail all this together with Tupac's raw racial politics, the Black Panther Party in his family tree, and his highly visible music and film careers, and you have a paradigm of the multidimensional Young Black Male: a seemingly impenetrable persona reeking of considerable talent, anger, charisma, ingenuity, and cockiness.

Tupac Shakur, a self-proclaimed "thug," is both a victim and symbol of today's violent climate. And this double role has media pundits, hip hop bashers, and black "spokespersons" scampering for explanations. Is Tupac's life imitating his art, or is it the other way around? Does rap music create and condone violence? And why are so-called gangsta rappers hailed as heroes by so many young people—black, brown, white, and otherwise?

The answers don't lie as much in Shakur's music as in his life. "What Tupac represents is considered alien by some," says his attorney Michael Warren, "because it speaks so bluntly to the harshest conditions of this society." These are conditions others would prefer to ignore. With his defiance and flair for high drama, Tupac is a symbol of black resistance, even if it's not always clear what it is he's resisting. His music is criticized for being "violent," but how does that differ from the larger pop culture and, by extension, America itself? The bullet-ridden messenger is being blamed for his bullet-ridden message. And if Tupac isn't really saying anything of any relevance, why do so many pay attention?

Tupac Shakur continues stomping on the lines between life and death, fame and infamy, blackness and Americanness, love and hate of women, and legal and illegal ways of expressing rage and torment. We would all do well to listen and watch. No matter how angry, violent, or bitter they may seem, the Tupacs of this country are telling us something. If we turn a deaf ear now, we'll most definitely hear the noise later. And it won't be on wax. *Kevin Powell*

As an artist, it's important for Tupac Shakur to express his beliefs and thoughts about life. Although we may not agree, we must respect his rights. There are a lot of things wrong in America today. When a voice speaks out, there is always someone waiting in the cut to shut him down. Tupac is one deep brother with many great talents. I believe he has been and can be a productive individual in our society. As for his criminal record, there are three sides to every story: his side, their side, and the truth.

Latoya T. Bryant
Raleigh, NC

"2Pacalypse Now," an update on Tupac's life and condition, confuses me. Kevin Powell says, "Tupac Shakur continues stomping on the lines between life and death, fame and infamy, blackness and Americanness . . . " continuing on, listing opposites. "Blackness" and "Americanness" are opposites? That's just wrong. A little advice: Watch what you're saying. Aren't we supposed to be promoting America as "blackness, whiteness, yellowness," etc.?

Fayerty Creagan
New York, NY

What we see in Tupac's shooting is how the gangsta mentality actually disrupts racial solidarity. Those other young black men who want to go out and destroy this talented young black man aren't operating from the ethos of racial solidarity that has been a tradition in rap.

bell hooks

READY TO LIVE

Make me wanna holler
The way they do my life
—Marvin Gaye

It was a chilly January morning when I made my way to Rikers Island for a conversation with Tupac Shakur, what would be his first words to any journalist since being shot last November 30. After passing through a series of checkpoints and metal detectors, I reached a dingy white conference room in the same building where Tupac was being held on $3 million bail. Within weeks, he'd receive a one-and-a-half- to four-and-a-half-year sentence for a sexual abuse conviction in his New York rape case.

Tupac strutted into the room without a limp, in spite of having been recently wounded in the leg—among other places. Dressed in a white Adidas sweatshirt and oversized blue jeans, he seemed more alert than he had been in all our interviews and encounters. He looked me in the eyes as we spoke and smoked one Newport after another. "I'm kinda nervous," he admitted at one point. After a brush with death and the barrage of rumor and innuendo that followed, Tupac said he'd summoned me because "this is my last interview. If I get killed, I want people to get every drop. I want them to have the real story."

How do you feel after everything you've been through these past few weeks?

Well, the first two days in prison, I had to go through what life is like when you've been smoking weed for as long as I have and then you stop. Emotionally, it was like I didn't know myself. I was sitting in a room, like there was two people in the room, evil and good. That was the hardest part. After that, the weed was out of me. Then every day I started doing, like, a thousand push-ups for myself. I was reading whole books in one day, and writing, and that was putting me in a peace of mind. Then I started seeing my situation and what got me here. Even though I'm innocent of the charge they gave me, I'm not innocent in terms of the way I was acting.

Could you tell me specifically what you mean?

I'm just as guilty for not doing nothing as I am for doing things. Not with this case, but just in my life. I had a job to do and I never showed up. I was so scared of this responsibility that I was running away from it. But I see now that whether I show up for work or not, the evil forces are going to be at me. They're going to come 100 percent, so if I don't be 100 percent pure-hearted, I'm going to lose. And that's why I'm losing.

When I got in here, all the prisoners was, like, "Fuck that gangsta rapper." I'm not a gangsta rapper. I rap about things that happen to me. I got shot five times, you know what I'm saying? People was trying to kill me. It was really real like that. I don't see myself being special; I just see myself having more responsibilities than the next man. People look to me to do things for them, to have answers. I wasn't

After the trial and the shooting and the media storm, Tupac Shakur is alive and well. He says Thug Life is dead, and that his new album, *Me Against the World,* may be his last, but Tupac's pulling no punches in this exclusive prison interview. *By Kevin Powell*

APRIL 1995

having them because my brain was half dead from smoking so much weed. I'd be in my hotel room, smoking too much, drinking, going to clubs, just being numb. That was being in jail to me. I wasn't happy at all on the streets. Nobody could say they saw me happy.

When we spoke a year ago, you said that if you ended up in jail, your spirit would die. You sound like you're saying the opposite now.

That was the addict speaking. The addict knew if I went to jail, then it couldn't live. The addict in Tupac is dead. The excuse maker in Tupac is dead. The vengeful Tupac is dead. The Tupac that would stand by and let dishonorable things happen is dead. God let me live for me to do something extremely extraordinary, and that's what I have to do. Even if they give me the maximum sentence, that's still my job.

Can you take us back to that night at Quad Recording Studios in Times Square?

The night of the shooting? Sure. Ron G. is a DJ out here in New York. He's, like, "Pac, I want you to come to my house and lay this rap down for my tapes." I said, "All right, I'll come for free." So I went to his house—me, Stretch, and a couple other homeboys. After I laid the song, I got a page from this guy Booker, telling me he wanted me to rap on Little Shawn's record. Now, this guy I was going to charge, because I could see that they was just using me, so I said, "All right, you give me seven G's and I'll do the song." He said, "I've got the money. Come." I stopped off to get some weed, and he paged me again. "Where you at? Why you ain't coming?" I'm, like, "I'm coming, man, hold on."

Did you know this guy?

I met him through some rough characters I knew. He was trying to get legitimate and all that, so I thought I was doing him a favor. But when I called him back for directions, he was, like, "I don't have the money." I said, "If you don't have the money, I'm not coming." He hung up the phone, then called me back: "I'm going to call [Uptown Entertainment CEO] Andre Harrell and make sure you get the money, but I'm going to give you the money out of my pocket." So I said, "All right, I'm on my way." As we're walking up to the building, somebody screamed from up the top of the studio. It was Little Caesar, Biggie's [the Notorious B.I.G.] sideman. That's my homeboy. As soon as I saw him, all my concerns about the situation were relaxed.

So you're saying that going into it . . .

I felt nervous because this guy knew somebody I had major beef with. I didn't want to tell the police, but I can tell the world. Nigel had introduced me to Booker. Everybody knew I was short on money. All my shows were getting canceled. All my money from my records was going to lawyers; all the movie money was going to my family. So I was rapping for guys and getting paid.

Who's this guy Nigel?

I was kicking it with him the whole time I was in New York doing *Above the Rim.* He came to me. He said, "I'm going to look after you. You don't need to get in no more trouble."

Doesn't Nigel also go by the name of Trevor?

Right. There's a real Trevor, but Nigel took on both aliases, you understand? So that's who I was kicking with—I got close to them.

If we really are saying rap is an art form, then we got to be more responsible for our lyrics. If you see everybody dying because of what you saying, it don't matter that you didn't make them die, it just matters that you didn't save them.

I used to dress in baggies and sneakers. They took me shopping; that's when I bought my Rolex and all my jewels. They made me mature. They introduced me to all these gangsters in Brooklyn, I met Nigel's family, went to his kid's birthday party—I trusted him, you know what I'm saying? I even tried to get Nigel in the movie, but he didn't want to be on film. That bothered me. I don't know any nigga that didn't want to be in the movies.

Who was with you the night of the shooting?

I was with my homeboy Stretch, his man Fred, and my sister's boyfriend, Zane. Not my bodyguard; I don't have a bodyguard. We get to the studio, and there's a dude outside in army fatigues with his hat low on his face. When we walked to the door, he didn't look up. I've never seen a black man not acknowledge me one way or the other, either with jealousy or respect. But this guy just looked to see who I was and turned his face down. It didn't click because I had just finished smoking some chronic. I'm not thinking something will happen to me in the lobby. While we're waiting to get buzzed in, I saw a dude sitting at a table reading a newspaper. He didn't look up either.

These are both black men?

Black men in their thirties. So first I'm, like, These dudes must be security for Biggie, because I could tell they were from Brooklyn from their army fatigues. But then I said, Wait a minute. Even Biggie's homeboys love me, why don't they look up? I pressed the elevator button, turned around, and that's when the dudes came out with the guns—two identical 9mms. "Don't nobody move. Everybody on the floor. You know what time it is. Run your shit." I was, like, What should I do?

I'm thinking Stretch is going to fight; he was towering over those niggas. From what I know about the criminal element, if niggas come to rob you, they always hit the big nigga first. But they didn't touch Stretch; they came straight to me. Everybody dropped to the floor like potatoes, but I just froze up. It wasn't like I was being brave or nothing; I just could not get on the floor. They started grabbing at me to see if I was strapped. They said, "Take off your jewels," and I wouldn't take them off. The light-skinned dude, the one that was standing outside, was on me. Stretch was on the floor, and the dude with the newspaper was holding the gun on him. He was telling the light-skin dude, "Shoot that motherfucker! Fuck it!" Then I got scared, because the dude had the gun to my stomach. All I could think about was piss bags and shit bags. I drew my arm around him to move the gun to my side. He shot and the gun twisted and that's when I got hit the first time. I felt it in my leg; I didn't know I got shot in my balls.

I dropped to the floor. Everything in my mind said, Pac, pretend you're dead. It didn't matter. They started kicking me, hitting me. I never said, "Don't shoot!" I was quiet as hell. They were snatching my shit off me while I was laying on the floor. I had my eyes closed, but I was shaking, because the situation had me shaking. And then I felt something on the back of my head, something real strong. I thought they stomped me or pistol-whipped me and they were stomping my head against the concrete. I saw white, just white. I didn't hear nothing, I didn't feel nothing, and I said, I'm unconscious. But I was conscious. And then I felt it again, and I could hear

things now and I could see things and they were bringing me back to consciousness. Then they did it again, and I couldn't hear nothing. And I couldn't see nothing; it was just all white. And then they hit me again, and I could hear things and I could see things and I knew I was conscious again.

Did you ever hear them say their names?

No. No. But they knew me, or else they would never check for my gun. It was like they were mad at me. I felt them kicking me and stomping me; they didn't hit nobody else. It was, like, "Ooh, motherfucker, ooh, aah"—they were kicking hard. So I'm going unconscious, and I'm not feeling no blood on my head or nothing. The only thing I felt was my stomach hurting real bad. My sister's boyfriend turned me over and said, "Yo, are you all right?" I was, like, "Yes, I'm hit, I'm hit." And Fred is saying he's hit, but that was the bullet that went through his leg.

So I stood up and I went to the door and—the shit that fucked me up—as soon as I got to the door, I saw a police car sitting there. I was, like, "Uh-oh, the police are coming, and I didn't even go upstairs yet." So we jumped in the elevator and went upstairs. I'm limping and everything, but I don't feel nothing. It's numb. When we got upstairs, I looked around, and it scared the shit out of me.

Why?

Because Andre Harrell was there, Puffy [Bad Boy Entertainment CEO Sean "Puffy" Combs] was there, Biggie . . . there was about forty niggas there. All of them had jewels on. More jewels than me. I saw Booker, and he had this look on his face like he was surprised to see me. I didn't know why. I had just beeped the buzzer and said I was coming upstairs.

Little Shawn bust out crying. I went, Why is Little Shawn crying, and I got shot? He was crying uncontrollably, like, "Oh my God, Pac, you've got to sit down!" I was feeling weird, like, Why do they want to make me sit down?

Because five bullets had passed through your body.

I didn't know I was shot in the head yet. I didn't feel nothing. I opened my pants, and I could see the gunpowder and the hole in my Karl Kani drawers. I didn't want to pull them down to see if my dick was still there. I just saw a hole and went, "Oh shit. Roll me some weed." I called my girlfriend and I was, like, "Yo, I just got shot. Call my mother and tell her."

Nobody approached me. I noticed that nobody would look at me. Andre Harrell wouldn't look at me. I had been going to dinner with him the last few days. He had invited me to the set of *New York Undercover*, telling me he was going to get me a job. Puffy was standing back too. I knew Puffy. He knew how much stuff I had done for Biggie before he came out.

So people did see blood on you?

They started telling me, "Your head! Your head is bleeding." But I thought it was just a pistol-whip. Then the ambulance came, and the police. First cop I looked up to see was the cop that took the stand against me in the rape charge. He had a half smile on his face, and he could see them looking at my balls. He said, "What's up, Tupac? How's it hanging?"

When I got to Bellevue Hospital, the doctor was going, "Oh my God!" I was, like, "What? What?" And I was hearing him tell other doctors, "Look at this. This is gunpowder right here." He was talking about my head: "This is the entry wound. This is the exit wound." And when he did that, I could actually feel the holes. I said, "Oh my God. I could feel that." It was the spots that I was blacking out on. And that's when I said, "Oh shit. They shot me in my head." They said, "You don't know how lucky you are. You got shot five times." It was, like, weird. I did not want to believe it. I could only remember that first shot, then everything went blank.

THIS IS MY LAST INTERVIEW. IF I GET KILLED, I WANT PEOPLE TO GET EVERY DROP. I WANT THEM TO GET THE REAL STORY.

At any point did you think you were going to die?

No. I swear to God. Not to sound creepy or nothing—I felt God cared for me from the first time the niggas pulled the gun out. The only thing that hurt me was that Stretch and them all fell to the floor. The bullets didn't hurt. Nothing hurt until I was recovering. I couldn't walk, I couldn't get up, and my hand was fucked up. I was looking on the news and it was lying about me.

Tell me about some of the coverage that bothered you.

The number one thing that bothered me was that dude that wrote that shit that said I pretended to do it. That I had set it up, it was an act. When I read that, I just started crying like a baby, like a bitch. I could not believe it. It just tore me apart.

And then the news was trying to say I had a gun and I had weed on me. Instead of saying I was a victim, they were making it like I did it.

What about all the jokes saying you had lost one of your testicles?

That didn't really bother me, because I was, like, Shit, I'm going to get the last laugh. Because I've got bigger nuts than all these niggas. My doctors are, like, "You can have babies." They told me that the first night, after I got exploratory surgery: "Nothing's wrong. It went through the skin and out the skin." Same thing with my head. Through my skin and out the skin.

Have you had a lot of pain since then?

Yes, I have headaches. I wake up screaming. I've been having nightmares, thinking they're still shooting me. All I see is niggas pulling guns, and I hear the dude saying, "Shoot that motherfucker!" Then I'll wake up sweaty as hell and I'll be, like, Damn, I have a headache. The psychiatrist at Bellevue said that's post-traumatic stress.

Why did you leave Bellevue Hospital?

I left Bellevue the next night. They were helping me, but I felt like a science project. They kept coming in, looking at my dick and shit, and this was not a cool position to be in. I knew my life was in danger. The Fruit of Islam was there, but they didn't have guns. I knew what type of niggas I was dealing with.

So I left Bellevue and went to Metropolitan. They gave me a phone and said, "You're safe here. Nobody knows you're here." But the phone would ring and someone would say, "You ain't dead yet?" I was, like, Damn! Those motherfuckers don't have no mercy. So I checked myself out, and my family took me to a safe spot, somebody who really cared about me in New York City.

Why did you go to court the morning after you were shot?

They came to the bed and said, "Pac, you don't need to go to court." I was, like, no. I felt like if the jury didn't see me, they would think I'm doing a show or some shit. Because they were sequestered and didn't know I got shot. So I knew I had to show up no matter what. I swear to God, the farthest thing from my mind was sympathy. All I could think of was, Stand up and fight for your life like you fight for your life in this hospital.

I sat there in a wheelchair, and the judge was not looking me in my eyes. He never looked me in my eyes the whole trial. So the jury came in, and the way everybody was acting, it was like a regular everyday thing. And I was feeling so miracle-ish that I'm living. And then I start feeling they're going to do what they're going to do. Then I felt numb; I said, I've got to get out of here.

When I left, the cameras were all rushing me and bumping into my leg and shit. I was, like, "You motherfuckers are like vultures." That made me see just the nastiest in the hearts of men. That's why I was looking like that in the chair when they were wheeling me away. I was trying to promise myself to keep my head up for all my people there. But when I saw all that, it made me put my head down; it just took my spirit.

Can we talk about the rape case at all?

Okay. Nigel and Trevor took me to Nell's. When we got there, I was immediately impressed, because it was different than any club I'd been in. It wasn't crowded, there was lots of space, there were beautiful women there. I was meeting Ronnie Lott from the New York Jets and Derrick Coleman from the Nets. They were coming up to me, like, "Pac, we're proud of you." I felt so tall that night, because they were people's heroes and they were saying I was their hero. I felt above and beyond, like I was glowing.

Somebody introduced me to this girl. And the only thing I noticed about her: She had a big chest. But she was not attractive; she looked dumpy, like. Money came to me and said, "This girl wants to do more than meet you." I already knew what that meant: She wanted to fuck. I just left them and went to the dance floor by myself. They were playing some Jamaican music, and I'm just grooving.

Then this girl came out and started dancing—and the shit that was weird, she didn't even come to me face-first, she came ass-first. So I'm dancing to this reggae music; you know how sensuous that is. She's touching my dick, she's touching my balls, she opened my zipper, she put her hands on me. There's a little dark part in Nell's, and I see people over there making out already, so she starts pushing me this way. I know what time it is.

We go over in the corner. She's touching me. I lift up my shirt while I'm dancing, showing off my tattoos and everything. She starts kissing my stomach, kissing my chest, licking me and shit. She's going down, and I'm, like, Oh shit. She pulled my dick out;

Tupac Shakur's third album, *Me Against the World,* is better than his first, *2Pacalypse Now,* and not quite as good as his second, *Strictly 4 My N.I.G.G.A.Z. Strictly* was an album of extremes—from the frantic shouts of "Holler If Ya Hear Me" to the glossy sexism of "I Get Around" to the swingy "Keep Ya Head Up." The ferociousness of Tupac's ire and his clearly spoken indignation were the thick threads that brought the album within a song or two of being a concept.

The new album is a mass of sad songs rapped over slow, sometimes plodding beats. Tupac lets go of his usual theme of thuggery-as-resistance, opting instead to consider his attraction to mood-altering substances like alcohol, weed, and guns. He ponders, on "If I Die 2Nite," whether "heaven got a ghetto for thug niggaz." By the final verse, he's hoarse, spitting words out like they taste bitter: "Don't shed a tear for me, nigga / I ain't happy here." It's an ice-cold song, way beyond blues.

But amid all his righteous venom, Pac, as is his practice, dispenses maxims. "Always do your best," he says over the bouncy music of the title song. "Don't let the pressure make you panic." In the ridiculously dull "Fuck the World," it's "Never take your eyes off the prize." He draws you in with these little do-

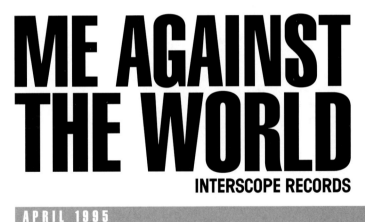

ME AGAINST THE WORLD

INTERSCOPE RECORDS

APRIL 1995

good moments—he seems, like this album, just schizo enough to be interesting, just crazy enough to be sincere.

Even as he tries to figure out whether women are tramp-ass bitches, damsels he can rescue, or moms he can revere; even as he raps of suicide and beatdowns; even when it's him—as he believes—against the world, Tupac can make hope sound as real as all the fucked-up shit. He proved it last time out—coming out of his mouth, the idea of keeping your head up doesn't sound corny at all.

Danyel Smith

I am the young woman that was sexually assaulted by Tupac Shakur and his thugs. I've read Kevin Powell's interview with Tupac, in which I was misrepresented. Up until

this point I have only told my story under oath in court; nobody has heard my story, only his side, which is much different than what Tupac stated is the true story.

A friend of mine took me to Nell's, where he introduced me to [the men VIBE identified as] Nigel and Trevor, who later introduced me to their friend Tupac. When I first met Tupac, he kissed me on my cheek and made small talk with me. After a while, I excused myself and started to walk to the dance floor. When I felt someone slide their hands into the back pocket of my jeans, I turned around, assuming it was my friend, but was shocked when I discovered it was Tupac. We danced for a while, and he touched my face and his body brushed mine. Due to the small dance floor and the large number of people, we were shoved into a dark corner. Tupac pulled up his shirt, took my hand, traced it down his chest, and sat it on top of his erect penis. He then kissed me and pushed my head down on his penis, and in a brief three-second encounter, my lips touched the head of his penis. This happened so suddenly that once I realized what he was trying to do, I swiftly brought my head up. I must reiterate that I did not suck his penis on the dance floor. He pulled his shirt back down and asked me what I was doing later. I told him that I was going home because I had to go to work that day. Then, as people started surrounding him again, he grabbed my arm and said, "Let's get out of here, I'm tired of people stressing me." We exited Nell's, got into a white BMW, pulled up at the Parker Meridien, and went to his

suite. We conversed, and he rolled up some blunts. We started kissing, and then we had oral and vaginal sexual intercourse several times.

He called my house a couple nights later and gave me his SkyPager number and told me he wanted to see me tomorrow. That evening after work, I paged him, and his road manager called me back and informed me that Pac really wanted to see me but he had a show to do in Jersey, so I should call a car service and take it to the Meridien and he would pay for the cab. Once I got to the hotel, I met Charles Fuller for the first time; he paid for the cab and led me upstairs. Inside the suite, Tupac, Nigel, and Trevor were seated in the living room, smoking weed and drinking Absolut. Tupac told me to come in and pointed to the arm of the sofa near him, and I sat down. After about twenty minutes, Tupac took my hand and led me into a bedroom in the suite. He fell onto the bed and asked me to give him a massage. So I massaged his

IT WAS NOT A SETUP. I NEVER KNEW ANY OF THE THUGS TUPAC WAS HANGING WITH. I ADMIT I DID NOT MAKE THE WISEST DECISIONS, BUT I DID NOT DESERVE TO BE GANG-RAPED.

back, he turned around, and I started massaging his chest.

Just as we began kissing, the door opened and I heard people entering. As I started to turn to see who it was, Tupac grabbed my head and told me, "Don't move." I looked down at him and he said, "Don't worry, baby, these are my brothers and they ain't going to hurt you. We do everything together." I started to shake my head, "No, no, Pac, I came here to be with you. I came here to see you. I don't want to do this." I started to rise up off the bed but he brutally

slammed my head down. My lips and face came crashing down hard onto his penis, he squeezed the back of my neck, and I started to gag. Tupac and Nigel held me down while Trevor forced his penis into my mouth. I felt hands tearing my shoes off, ripping my stockings and panties off. I couldn't move; I felt paralyzed, trapped, and I started to black out. They leered at my body. "This bitch got a fat ass, she's fine." While they laughed and joked to one another, Nigel, Trevor, and Fuller held me in the room, trying to calm me down. They would not allow me to leave.

Finally, I got to the elevators, which had a panel of mirrors. Once I caught sight of myself, I sank down on the floor and started to cry. They came out, picked me up, and brought me back into the suite. Tupac was lying on the couch. In my mind I'm thinking, "This motherfucker just raped me, and he's lying up here like a king acting as if nothing happened." So I began crying hysterically and shouting, "How could you do this to me? I came here to see you. I can't believe you did this to me." Tupac replied, "I don't have time for this shit. Get this bitch out of here."

The aforementioned is the true story. It was not a setup, and I never knew any of the thugs he was hanging with. Tupac knows exactly what he did to me. I admit I did not make the wisest decisions, but I did not deserve to be gang-raped.

Name Withheld
New York, NY

We received an overwhelming response to the VIBE Q with Tupac Shakur ["Ready to Live" by Kevin Powell, April '95]. Several of the people mentioned in the interview were contacted before the story was published but declined to comment at that time. After the interview appeared, they contacted VIBE, wanting to respond to what they felt were misconceptions that arose from some of Tupac's statements and descriptions. Here are excerpts from their replies, as told to Fab 5 Freddy.

ANDRE HARRELL

That night when I went to the studio, there were three sessions going on. There was Little Shawn's session, then upstairs SWV was happening, and on the other floor Biggie Smalls [The Notorious B.I.G.] was doing his thing. Hope was in the air and success was all around. Everybody was all excited about Pac comin' in, but we were starting to get antsy because he was supposed to get there at a certain time, and we wanted to see how this song with Little Shawn was going to set off.

When he got off the elevator, we were all standing in the hall. Tupac was just bopping back and forth saying, "I was set up." At first I didn't realize he had been shot, because he wasn't bleeding heavily from the head. It looked like he had had a fight. He said, "It's not goin' down like that." I was, like, "Yo, Money, you shot. You need to sit down." He told Stretch to roll him up a spliff. He was in movie mode at this point. He did the whole James Cagney thing.

I said, "Let's call the ambulance." I was basically the one who was taking care of the police and the ambulance people. I wasn't making any calls; I was directing the studio exactly who to call, so I was talking more to Stretch because the paramedics were looking at Pac. There was no need for me to look at the wound.

I remember telling Stretch, "You got to go with him." 'Cause I wasn't trusting the police with Tupac. He had too many open issues with the police. I was feeling like something could have happened between the ride and the hospital. I ended up staying in the studio till four in the morning, 'cause the police interviewed everybody and wouldn't let anybody leave. I tried to call the hospital when I was walking out of the studio to see if I could go by there. They said they were looking at him and nobody could see him.

I was glad Tupac said he was basically through with the whole bad-guy image and that he wants to redirect his energy. So I guess there was some level of positivity that came out from all this. I want to go and see Pac and just talk to him, see where his head is at. 'Cause he knows what's real and what's not, and in the quietness of his mind, you know, he's dealing with all the truth. And for me, that's almost enough.

THE NOTORIOUS B.I.G.

I had a session with the Junior Mafia at Quad Studios. Little Ceez and Meno and all them was on the little terrace they got out there, smoking weed. They was looking around and they saw Stretch and Pac and all them niggas pull up. We all family, so niggas greeted each other from upstairs to downstairs. Next thing you know, everybody was, like, "Yo, Pac just got shot." So I'm on my way downstairs, no gat, to see what's up with my man. Everybody holding me back.

I get downstairs and everything's on some lockdown shit. Nobody moves. Immediately, police thought everybody in the studio was on the same floor where everything was supposed to have happened at. I saw Pac get out on a stretcher, but when he actually came out from the elevator, I wasn't even there.

When I read the interview I felt like he was just shitting on everybody. I always said that he was the realest nigga in the game. I don't know what he was trying to hide, or if he was scared. I figured that with the shit he was talking in VIBE, he was just confused more than anything. You get shot and then you go to jail for something you ain't even do—that could twist a nigga's mind up.

And then the story just completely got switched around: niggas saying I set him up and I'm the one that got him shot. They're saying that my record "Who Shot Ya?" is about him. That shit is crazy. That song was finished way before Tupac got shot. Niggas was takin' little pieces of the song and trying to add it to the story, and that shit is crazy. Other niggas look at that VIBE piece, like, "Damn, Little Caesar was on the terrace. He must have been the lookout man." And it's real niggas in the streets thinking, "That's fucked up, what B.I.G. did to Tupac." I think that should be erased. Never, ever in life.

As far as with me, he always gonna be my man, even when I go see him again. But he need to just check himself. And I want an apology. 'Cause I don't get down like that.

BOOKER

There was a lot of people passing through the studio that night, and the word definitely got out that Tupac was on his way. We were waiting on Tupac for hours. Next thing I know, about 12:00, Tupac comes off the elevator. It looked like he just got in a scuffle. Then I seen the blood on his head. He was pacing back and forth, hysterically, talking about "Call the police, call the police." Then he looked at me and said, "You the only one who knew that I was coming. You must've set me up." I was, like, "Yo, you buggin', Tupac. C'mere and talk to me." He kept pacing back and forth, and saying, "Call the police." He never said to call the ambulance.

In the paper he said he'd been set up, that he knew the assailants and blazey-boom. But everybody in the industry knew that he came off the elevator saying, "You set me up." I thought me and him was some kind of friends. But I felt maybe this was a strategy for him to

HE'S BELIEVING HIS RAP. HE'S BELIEVING THE MOVIE SCRIPTS THAT HE'S PLAYED. WHERE HE WENT WRONG WAS WHEN HE TRIED TO GO TO THE STREET.

THE STORY JUST GOT COMPLETELY SWITCHED AROUND: THEY'RE SAYING THAT MY RECORD "WHO SHOT YA?" IS ABOUT HIM. THAT'S CRAZY. THE SONG WAS FINISHED WAY BEFORE TUPAC GOT SHOT.

get around his case. And maybe I shouldn't hold him accountable for trying that strategy.

But after the VIBE interview, I seen that this nigga is using the media to get his point across and look like he had the upper hand. He made it seem like niggas had a plot against him. Like he was so important that street niggas wanted to kill him, industry niggas wanted to kill him. He's believing his rap. He's believing the movie scripts that he's played. Where he went wrong was when he tried to go to the street, and when it came down to the test, he did not hold up. He's gonna assassinate people's character, saying that niggas was crying and falling to the floor like a sack of potatoes. It just goes to show that the real coward and the real nigga that was crying was Tupac.

LITTLE SHAWN

All I know is that Money was supposed to come and he agreed to do the song with me. When I got there, it was like a fucking party. I ain't really keen on a whole bunch of people in the studio while I'm working. I don't know how, but everybody must have known this cat was comin'.

Then the elevator goes ding. Money gets off the elevator and starts yelling, "Ah! I got shot. Nigga set me up. Muthafucka shot me; they shot Tupac." The back of his head was busted open and it was bleeding all down his face. He caught everybody by surprise. For like only a split second, until the shock wore off, nobody really wanted to fuck with him because he was jumping around like an animal.

Reading the interview and being there, nothing made sense. He said Andre didn't want to look at him, Puffy didn't want to look at him. He's trying to state that nobody paid him any mind? Come on, man. I don't know this dude from a hole in the wall, and I was trying to help him. He said, "Little Shawn was crying uncontrollably." You sound like an idiot saying some dumb shit like that. When I was helping him, he didn't say, "You cryin' like a bitch. Get away from me." I was surprised that Money even had the audacity to go there. I've punched a lot of people in their mouth behind that "Little Shawn was cryin'" shit.

Then I hear everybody is saying that I had something to do with it. And niggas on the West Coast are saying, "Yo, tell that nigga Little Shawn to be careful. 'Cause niggas on the West Coast is calling his name." I don't need that in my life. A lot of people go through problems with the law, and that ain't nothing to be glorified. Every time this dude gets arrested, it's in the paper because of who he is, but he's loving it. I ain't no media gangster. That dude is Media Man. He is ridiculous.

SEAN "PUFFY" COMBS

Basically, the whole thing must have been a dream. We were shooting Biggie's "Warning" video, and I see one of the Bad Boy staff members on his way to Biggie's session. I knew that Biggie had a session with Junior Mafia, but I didn't know it was right around the corner. So I'm going to check B.I.G., you know what I'm saying?

When I get off the elevator at Quad, you have to stop in a reception area, and there's this Little Shawn session with Andre. So I stopped to say "What's up?" to them. I'm about to go up to Biggie's session when Pac comes out the elevator and he's shot up. He had some blood coming out of his head, but there wasn't a lot of blood. He was holding his groin area and limping a little bit.

Nobody turned their backs on him; niggas was all up on him. Immediately, Andre was, like, "Oh my God, call the ambulance." Tupac wanted to go to the phone, so me and my man Groovy Lou was by his side, trying to hold him up, getting him to calm down. He was telling Groovy Lou to roll him a blunt. He definitely brought the theatrics to it.

He got a lot of people in a lot of bullshit with that interview. The way it was written, it was open-ended, like me and B.I.G. and Andre had something to do with it. I would never, ever purposely try to hurt no next man. That man had his own beefs with niggas. I ain't never had no beef with that man.

I hope that his Thug Life shit is really over. But on the real, if you gonna be a motherfuckin' thug, you gots to live and die a thug, you know what I'm sayin'? There ain't no jumpin' in and out of thugism. If that's what you choose to do, you gots to go out like that. I ain't no thug. Only thugs I know is dead or in jail. Or about to be.

Even still, I ain't got no beef. I pray for him, and it's all good. I'm writing him a letter. I want to hear what he's thinking face to face. Out of everybody, I'm the easiest to forgive. I've been there where the whole press is against you, the world ain't understanding you, niggas don't know what really went on. And you get confused. That's the only thing I can see is confusion.

STRETCH

Me and Pac have been down from day one. Before he did *Juice*, before his first album. That's my man. So the interview he did in VIBE bugged me out. But I know him. He likes to talk a lot. Especially when he's upset, he'll say shit that he won't even mean. And then he'll think about it later and be, like, "Damn, why the fuck did I say that?"

We was kinda skeptical when we was going to the studio. We was,

Tupac has to take responsibility for his actions or lack of the same. He should have done something besides leaving that woman in a compromising position in a room full of men. Black men are going to have to learn to assert themselves and challenge other black men by stopping them when it comes to harming our women. The test is, if you wouldn't allow this to happen to your mother or sister, why sit by and allow it to happen to any other woman? Black men have to stop condoning the negative behavior of their brothers even if it makes them look soft.

Carol Richardson
Carson, CA

Tupac has learned more about himself than he has ever known, now that he is not smoking bud or drinking. Many of my homies met him and said he was a straight punk or an asshole because he disrespected almost everyone he came across and he was only acting hard because that was his image. But hearing him say that he was always under the influence and that he shouldn't have been acting that way, I guess he now realizes his mistakes.

Veronica Castillo
Inglewood, CA

C'mon, people. Tupac's talking that same ol' jailhouse bullshit that all niggas locked up are always talking about. The bottom line is that if Tupac hadn't gotten locked up, his ass would've still been out here doing the same foul shit he was doing before. He strikes me as just another phony nigga trying to be hard like every other gangsta out here. Tupac needs to start being his own leader and stop following behind other motherfuckers. He gets no sympathy, respect, or props from me!

Gisel P.
New York, NY

With Tupac being incarcerated, I understand what he must be going through, because I am also incarcerated. Here's a poem of encouragement I wrote for him:

KEEP YA HEAD UP, 2PAC
To the rapper who makes much sense, 2Pac Shakur don't you ever quit. Life has its obstacles, God knows it does, with the rhymes you wrote it showed much love. Some were positive and some were life as we saw it on the streets that we fight. Now it's time to do your thing, get it together, come out and say: It's a new me now, I've saw the light, I must help my young brothers and sisters to save their life. I'm proud of you and the changes you've made, stick with your word, stay strong and brave.

Amira Bush
Goochland, VA

ME (AND HER) AGAINST THE WORLD

Cue the "Wedding March" sample: Tupac Shakur, once rap's ruling bachelor, is getting around no more. On April 29, Shakur wedded longtime girlfriend Keisha Morris in upstate New York's Clinton Correctional Facility, where the rapper is serving eighteen months to four and a half years for sexual abuse. Attendance was limited by prison officials, but Morris's mother and a cousin of Tupac witnessed the ceremony.

AUGUST 1995

Morris and Shakur met over a year earlier in a New York club, and had wedding plans before Tupac's November '94 trial (in which he was accused of raping a woman he'd met in a different New York club). Morris, a prelaw student, apparently wasn't dismayed by Tupac's incarceration and previous brushes with the law. "The way they feel about each other hasn't changed, despite the circumstances," says a source close to both parties. "They believe in each other, and they believe they'll have a bright future together."

Josh Tyrangiel

What is the purest measure of juice you ever tasted?

Everything from seeing Tupac get out of prison and Snoop Dogg beating his murder trial to being able to walk the streets of any ghetto and still live in Compton.
— *Suge Knight*

HIT MAN

Suge Knight might make Death Row Records the Motown of the '90s—as long as he can keep his stars, and himself, out of prison. *By Allison Samuels*

On a typically breezy Southern California night, music exec Marion "Suge" Knight Jr. is out cruising the boulevards of Los Angeles, posse in tow. Sporting a sparkling two-carat diamond earring, brand-new leather Filas, and a UCLA baseball cap, Knight makes his way to a trendy East L.A. nightclub. Upon arrival, the six-foot-four, 315-pound former defensive end has no problem navigating through the thick dance floor crowd. As he passes, an awed club patron says out loud to no one in particular, "That Suge Knight ain't no motherfucking joke."

In true Berry Gordy style, the name Suge Knight has become synonymous with megabuck deals, superstar careers, and platinum albums. And in true OG style, Knight's name has also become synonymous with some of the most frightening tales of threats, gunplay, and beatdowns the music industry has ever known. As the 29-year-old CEO of Death Row Records, Knight and his partner, producer extraordinaire Dr. Dre, have turned the record biz upside down with their Midas touch on the charts—and Suge's alleged heavy touch on anyone who gets in Death Row's way.

The drama began four years ago when the late Eric "Eazy-E" Wright filed suit, claiming Knight and two others assaulted him with pipes and bats to get Dre released from a contract with Wright's Ruthless Records. Though the suit was later dismissed, Knight's reputation as the wrong nigga to fuck with kept rolling. It has now reached mythic status with the in-your-face success of Death Row, worth an estimated $100 million. Plans for the label's future depend on the outcome of Snoop Doggy Dogg's murder trial, Dre's halfway house stint, and Suge's own problems.

The Compton native dismisses all the talk that paints him as a black prototype for the next Scorsese gangsta flick. "The rumors are helpful but not true," says the surprisingly mild-mannered Knight. "They get me additional respect, and this business is about getting the respect you deserve so you can get what you want. I don't worry about all the talk."

But Knight's got more than talk to contend with. He was recently sentenced to five years' probation for assault charges brought by two aspiring rappers who say, among other things, that Knight pulled out a gun and beat them over the use of a recording studio phone. Though federal agents are investigating, the law's not his only problem; word on the street is that there are three contracts out on his life right now.

Rumors and court cases notwithstanding, Knight's current sweet life of stretch limousines, $1,000 hotel suites, and a very expensive car collection is worlds away from the modest two-bedroom house where he grew up with his mom, dad, and two older sisters. His father, a Mississippi-born truck driver, encouraged Suge (so named for his sugary-sweet disposition) to make his name on the football field—not the music charts. But after being named UNLV's rookie of the year, hopes of NFL stardom got him only as far as tryouts with the Los Angeles Rams. "I love the game and still play from time to time," he says. "But it wasn't meant to be. So I moved on."

Unfortunately, "moving on" led to the beginning of a long series of run-ins with the LAPD. But after forming a small music publishing company, Knight hooked up with Vanilla Ice just before Ice's hugely—if briefly—successful debut album. When it came time to be paid, though, Knight almost got the shaft. "But I didn't let that happen," he says with a sly smile. "You can get fucked real quick in this industry if you don't know what's going on."

Knight's quickly acquired publishing knowledge led to discussions with the D.O.C. and Andre "Dr. Dre" Young about their contracts at Ruthless Records. After reading their agreements (which Knight describes as "real fucked-up"), he urged them to raise up out of Eazy's company. With a "nice piece of change" in his pocket, courtesy of his publishing ventures, Knight personally bankrolled the $250,000 cost of Dr. Dre's album, *The Chronic,* and he and Dre eventually connected with Interscope Records to back their Death Row label.

Knight hopes an oft-postponed Death Row tour (including Snoop, Dre, the Lady of Rage, Jewell, and Tha Dogg Pound) will finally take place this year. Knight, who also acts as a "consultant" to Uptown recording artists Mary J. Blige and Jodeci, rejects the notion that his rep might scare away potential business and destroy his dream of Death Row becoming the Motown of the '90s. "I'm in this game to win, and that means playing the best way you know how," he says.

SEPTEMBER 1995

"There are no hard-and-fast rules in the industry—no rights or wrongs. As long as you're bringing in the money, they will deal with you, no matter what anybody says."

Away from Death Row, Knight can be found keeping his no-fat physique toned at a local gym. Or you may peep him on Crenshaw Avenue engaging in his other favorite pastime: flipping switches in one of his "six-fours." Last year, he and Dre further expanded their entrepreneurial empire when they opened Let Me Ride Hydraulics, a custom lowrider shop that employs fifteen young men from the 'hood. Also on the agenda is another celebration for South Central mothers, whom Knight transports to Beverly Hills for a candlelit, five-course Mother's Day champagne brunch. This year Death Row shelled out about $75,000 for the event.

Reaching for the next level, Knight is also looking to publish his own music magazine and give Spike a run for his money by producing feature films with Dr. Dre under the Death Row umbrella. Their first venture, a $75,000, 18-minute short film based on Snoop's *Murder Was the Case,* got props from director Oliver Stone and sparked a multiplatinum soundtrack.

"My mission is helping young black talent see their dreams happen," says Knight. "That's my ultimate purpose in this business, so fuck anybody who can't understand or deal with that. I know how I am and what my heart is like," he says slowly. "I leave my judgment to God."

DEATH ROW

Suge Knight has the muscle. Dr. Dre has the skills. And with Snoop, Tha Dogg Pound, and now Tupac, Death Row Records has the music industry all shook up.
By Kevin Powell

LIVE FROM

But some man will say, How are the dead raised up?

And with what body do they come?

—1 Corinthians 15:35

No one can just drop in on Death Row Records CEO Marion "Suge" Knight Jr. without feeling the magnitude of his reputation. No one.

On a cool Southern California evening, I arrive to see him at the Can-Am Building in Tarzana, a thirty-minute drive north of Los Angeles. I'm greeted by a tall, stone-faced, caramel-colored man with a walkie-talkie and a black windbreaker inscribed SECURITY. Rather than letting me into the tiny lobby area, he tells me to wait outside while he alerts someone within the single-story edifice that Suge has a visitor.

The budding legend surrounding 30-year-old Suge Knight is such that damn near everyone—from fellow journalists to former and current Death Row employees all the way to a shoeshine man in West L.A.—warned me that Suge was "the wrong nigga to fuck with." The mere mention of his name was enough to cause some of the most powerful people in the music business to whisper, change the subject, or beg to be quoted off the record.

This is an especially hectic time for Knight and Death Row, whose "keepin' it real" mentality has the industry all shook up. Tha Dogg Pound's controversial debut album, *Dogg Food*—the breaking point in the relationship between Time Warner and Interscope Records, Death Row's distributor—was finally released last Halloween and shot to number one on the pop charts. As Snoop Doggy Dogg faced a murder charge in L.A., Knight secured a $1.4 million bond to bail Tupac Shakur out of prison in October and signed him up (both to Death Row Records and Knight's management arm). Shakur has been working feverishly on his Death Row debut—a double CD all written since Shakur's release, titled *All Eyez on Me* (twenty-eight cuts, including a duet with Snoop called "Two of America's Most Wanted")—partly because a return to prison still looms, pending appeals.

Meanwhile, work continues with singers Danny Boy and Nate Dogg, and rappers the Lady of Rage, Jewell, Sam Sneed, and others yet unheard of—to say nothing of the artists for whom Knight now "consults," including Mary J. Blige, Jodeci, and DJ Quik. Death Row is also backing record labels headed by Snoop (Doggystyle Records) and Tha Dogg Pound (Gotta Get Somewhere Records). Plus there's Knight's new Club 662 in Las Vegas and the vision of Dr. Dre directing movies for Death Row Films.

All these things are on my mind as I'm being frisked in the lobby of the Can-Am Building, now the permanent studio for Death Row, where talents as diverse as Bobby Brown, Harry Belafonte, and Barry Manilow once recorded. Around-the-clock protection is provided by a group of off-duty black police officers who work in Los Angeles. While Death Row isn't the group's only client, it's the biggest. According to the guard at the reception desk, "We're better security because we're all licensed to carry guns—anywhere."

Another tall, muscular black man escorts me back to Suge's office—the building also contains two state-of-the-art studios, a gym, and a space where Suge often sleeps. The man opens the door, and I'm struck by two things: a big, light-brown German shepherd rolling on the floor, and the fact that virtually everything in the room—the carpet, the cabinets, the sofa and matching chairs—is a striking blood red. I look at my escort; he reads my facial expression and says nonchalantly, "That's Damu. He won't bother you. He's only trained to kill on command." On that note, I step gingerly into Suge Knight's office.

Knight's imprint is all over: from the sleek stereo system to the air conditioner (set way too cold) to the large-screen TV that doubles as an all-seeing security monitor. Right in front of his big wooden desk, outlined in white on the red carpet, is the Death Row Records logo: a man strapped to an electric chair with a sack over his head. I was told by another journalist that no one steps on the logo. No one.

Sporting a close-cropped haircut and a neatly trimmed beard, Knight strikes a towering pose. When he sits down to face me, with Damu (Swahili for "blood") now lying by his feet, you can't help but notice the huge biceps itching to bust through his red-and-black-striped shirt. Muscle, say both his admirers and detractors, is the name of Knight's game. Speaking with a syrupy drawl, Suge (as in "sugar") details the original mission of Death Row Records.

"First thing to do was to establish an organization, not just no record company," he says, his eyes looking straight into mine. "I knew the difference between having a record company and having a production company and a logo. First goal was to own our masters. Without your master tapes you ain't got shit, period."

As Knight speaks of Dr. Dre's *The Chronic*, which laid the foundation for Death Row in 1992, and Snoop's solo debut, *Doggystyle*, which proved that Death Row was more than just a vanity label, I can't help but notice how utterly simple and ghetto—in the sense that the underclass has always done what it takes to survive—his logic is. Ain't no complicated equations or middle-class maneuvers here, just, according to Knight, people getting what they deserve. And never forgetting where they come from.

"We called it Death Row 'cause most everybody had been involved with the law," Knight explains. "A majority of our people was parolees or incarcerated—it's no joke. We got people really was on death row and still is."

Indeed, there is no way to truly comprehend the incredible success of Death Row Records—its estimated worth now tops $100 million—without first understanding the conditions that created the rap game in the first place: few legal economic paths in America's inner cities, stunted educational opportunities, a pervasive sense of alienation among young black males, black folks' age-old need to create music, and a typically American hunger for money and power.

The Hip Hop Nation is no different than any other segment of this society in its desire to live the American dream. Hip hop, for better or for worse, has been this generation's most prominent means for making good on the long-lost promises of the civil rights movement. However, the big question is, Where does this pull-yourself-up-by-your-bootstraps economic nationalism end and the high drama that hovers over Death Row Records begin?

The music industry thrives on rumors, and Death Row is always grist for the gossip mill. Stories run the gamut from Knight and his boys using metal pipes in persuading the late Eazy-E to release Dr. Dre from Ruthless Records, to former Uptown CEO Andre Harrell being strong-armed into restructuring Mary J. Blige's and Jodeci's contracts, to an alleged beef between Knight and Bad Boy Entertainment CEO Sean "Puffy" Combs, which some trace to the shooting death of one of Knight's close friends last October.

That incident, some say, has fueled a growing East Coast versus West Coast battle, and—so go the rumors—has led to reported threats on Combs's life. "I heard there was a contract out on my life," says Combs. "Why do they have so much hatred for me? I ask myself that question every day. I'm ready for them to leave me alone, man."

In an interview in last April's VIBE, Shakur suggested that Combs, the Notorious B.I.G., Shakur's longtime friend Randy "Stretch" Walker, and others behaved suspiciously immediately following Shakur's shooting in New York on November 30, 1994. Exactly one year to the day after Shakur's shooting, Walker was murdered execution-style in Queens. (When contacted by phone after the murder, Shakur offered no comment.)

The drama had already intensified when Knight bailed out Shakur last October and brought him to Death Row. Shakur's "relentless" new double album for Death Row includes a track featuring Faith Evans—one of Combs's artists and Biggie Smalls's wife—titled "Wonder Why They Call You Bitch." According to one source, "Tupac and Faith are now very, very close." ("Me and Faith don't have no problems," says Shakur. When asked about their relationship beyond the studio, he replies, "I ain't gonna answer that shit, man. You know I don't kiss and tell.") While Knight has said repeatedly that he wants Death Row to be "the Motown of the '90s," the label's history is unfolding more like an in-your-face Martin Scorsese film than Berry Gordy's charm school approach.

I ask Knight about all the rumors. He shifts his weight in his chair and bristles. "When you become the best, it's more rumors, it's more people want to stop you, 'cause everybody want to be number one."

"Can we talk about any of these alleged incidents?"

"Say what you want to say."

I then recount my understanding of the Andre Harrell story as Knight stares at me. Before long, he's flipped the script, asking me what I would do if I wasn't receiving a fair deal.

"You should get the best deal you can get in this business," I respond.

Knight edges forward in his chair, proud he got me to agree. "See, people got this business mixed up," he says. "They want to go and talk about a person who fixin' to come and help you. They don't say nothin' about the motherfucker who beatin' people out they money."

When you stand up for right, people should tip they hat to you and keep movin', and mind they own business."

Not totally satisfied with Knight's response, I wonder why rappers the D.O.C. and RBX are no longer with Death Row Records, and why both have gone on record, literally, complaining of not being paid. But Knight's already defensive, and I don't want to get tossed out before I get to bring up other, more important questions.

"What about the methods you used to get Harrell to renegotiate those contracts?" I ask.

"It's like this. Was you there?"

"Nah."

"Then there's nothin' to talk about."

What Knight will talk about is how important it is for him and Death Row to stay rooted in the streets. The youngest of three children and a proud native of working-class Compton (where he still keeps a house), Knight was a star defensive lineman in high school and at the University of Nevada at Las Vegas before entering the music business in the late 1980s. It's not clear how he got into the game—some say he was the D.O.C.'s bodyguard during the N.W.A days, while Knight maintains he started a music publishing business that earned a small fortune off Vanilla Ice's smash 1990 debut. Whatever the case, few individuals have as much drive as Knight: "Ghetto politics teaches

IF IT KEEPS GOING THIS WAY, PRETTY SOON NIGGAS FROM THE EAST COAST AIN'T GONNA BE ABLE TO COME OUT HERE AND BE SAFE. AND VICE VERSA.

you how to win and really be hungry. I never been the one who wanted to work with nobody. 'Cause I think if a motherfucker get you a paycheck—listen to how it sound, paycheck, like they paying you to stay in check. Can't nobody keep me in check."

Time Warner couldn't. It bowed to political pressure and announced it was selling its 50 percent interest in Death Row's profitable distributor, Interscope Records. Self-appointed gangsta rap watchdog C. DeLores Tucker couldn't. She may have helped get Interscope dropped, but she had no effect on Death Row's progress. In fact, at one point she met with Knight to get a piece of the action. He turned her down.

Despite all the community outreach Suge Knight does—the lavish Mother's Day dinners for single mothers, the turkey giveaways at Thanksgiving, the Christmas toy giveaways for Compton children—he has to know he puts fear in some hearts, that his I-don't-give-a-fuck persona unfurls itself long before people ever meet him in the flesh. Hip hop has always been about being straight-up, about being skeptical of the motives of the generation ahead of us, about creating shields (or myths) to protect our world from outsiders—Bob Dole, William Bennett, C. DeLores Tucker—who seek to come in and dom-

inate us. With four-year-old Death Row Records as his sword and an aura Al Pacino's Scarface would be proud of, Suge Knight epitomizes that mind-set—but at what cost?

Listen to Knight summarize his modus operandi: "Black executives, they get invited to the golf tournaments. I don't give a fuck about all that. I'm not gonna play golf with you. When you playin' golf, I'ma be in the studio. While you trying to eat dinner with the other executives in the business, I'ma be havin' dinner with my family, which is the artists on the label." He pauses to emphasize his point. "Without your talent, you ain't shit."

Talent is something 30-year-old Grammy winner Dr. Dre, né Andre Young, has in abundance. On a different day in the Can-Am Building's studio A, hip hop's most sought-after producer is waiting for Tupac to show up and continue work on his new album. The Compton-born cofounder (with Knight) and president of Death Row, Dr. Dre has sold fifteen million records in the past decade. Six foot one, 200-plus pounds, Dre wears a beige Fila outfit, brown Timberlands, and a gold Rolex saturated with diamonds. If that isn't enough, a chunk of diamond and gold glitters on one of his fingers. Those adornments aside, I'm surprised how soft-spoken and shy the baby-faced Dr. Dre is in person, his eyes avoiding mine for much of the interview. To break the ice, I ask about the World Class Wreckin' Cru, his first group back in the early 1980s.

"Wreckin' Cru was a DJ crew. They used to call it that because it was the guys that came in after the party was over and broke down the equipment," Dre says, leaning closer to my tape recorder as he warms to the topic.

"We eventually made a record, and we had the costumes on and what have you. Back then, everybody had their little getups, you know, like SoulSonic Force, UTFO." Dre laughs at the memory. "That shit haunted me, but you know, I ain't ashamed of my past."

Dre grew disillusioned with the Wreckin' Cru's style and teamed up with a teenage rapper named Ice Cube. They performed live at clubs and skating rinks. "We used to take people's songs, you know, and change them and make them dirty. Like 'My Adidas' was—" Dre laughs hard from the gut up. "Cube had this thing called 'My Penis.' We rocked it, and people would go crazy. So we just took that and started making records with it. And with me being a DJ, I used to sit in the club during the week and make up beats just to play in the club. I would take somebody else's song and re-create it and make it an instrumental. So that's how I basically got into producing."

Eventually Dre decided to form a group, but he needed a financial backer. In 1986, he met Eric "Eazy-E" Wright, a former drug dealer and fellow Compton resident looking to pump his money into something legal. Dre produced an Eazy single called "Boyz-N-the Hood," and it was on. "We hustled the record every day for eight months," says Dre, "riding around in a jeep, selling it from record store to record store ourselves."

DJ Yella, an old Wreckin' Cru partner, joined Dre, Eazy, Cube, MC Ren, and short-term member Arabian Prince to form arguably the most influential rap act ever. N.W.A's 1989 landmark, *Straight Outta Compton,* introduced an entire nation to urban blight, West Coast style. The album, produced largely by Dr. Dre and released on the underground label Ruthless Records, went double platinum with virtually no radio play. Dre says he and Eazy started Ruthless, although it was Eazy and Jerry Heller—a middle-aged white man who'd previously worked with Elton John and Pink Floyd—who gained credit for building America's first multimillion-dollar hardcore rap label.

Despite his meteoric success, Dre grows bitter when describing the disintegration of Ruthless Records and his relationship with Eazy-E. "The split came when Jerry Heller got involved," he recalls. "He played the divide-and-conquer game. He picked one nigga to take care of, instead of taking care of everybody, and that was Eazy. And Eazy was just, like, 'Well, shit, I'm taken care of, so fuck it.'"

When I reach Heller later by telephone, he reluctantly admits that Dre "was probably right. You know, Dre was a producer and a member of the group," he says. "Eazy was interested in being Berry Gordy, so more of my time was spent with Eazy."

During the production of N.W.A's *Efil4zaggin* album, Dre decided he wanted out of his contract. He almost spits out the recollection: "I was gettin' like two points for my production on albums. I still have the contracts framed." Dre adjusts his Rolex. "I'm not no egotistical person. I just want what I'm supposed to get. Not a penny more, not a penny less."

That's where Knight came in. "Suge brought it to my attention that I was being cheated," he says. "I wanted to do my own thing anyway. I was going to do it with Ruthless, but there was some sheisty shit, so I had to get ghost." Exactly how Knight helped Dre "get ghost" depends on whom you ask. When I mention to Jerry Heller that Knight maintains he's never threatened or beaten up anyone to make a gain in the music business, Heller cracks an eerie laugh reminiscent of Vincent Price's on Michael Jackson's *Thriller,* then says, "I would say he's taking poetic license."

Dre gives Knight credit for coming up with the plan for Death Row in 1991. He assures me he and Knight are "fifty-fifty partners. You know, me and Suge, we like brothers and shit." These two buddies figured Dr. Dre's name was bankable enough to start a record label and get a distribution deal, but unbelievably, there were no takers at first. Finally Interscope took a chance and Death Row (the label was going to be called Future Shock, after an old Curtis Mayfield single, until Dre and Knight purchased the more dramatic handle from one of Dre's homeboys) has become the most profitable independently owned African-American hip hop label of the 1990s.

Death Row's first release, *The Chronic,* dissed Eazy-E and Jerry Heller numerous times. But when conversation turns to Eazy's death from AIDS last March, Dre grows solemn. "I didn't believe it till I went to the hospital." He sighs, rubs his chin, and collects his thoughts. "He looked normal. That's what makes the shit so fuckin' scary, man. But he was unconscious, so he didn't even know I was there." Obviously, adds Dre, the ensuing battle over ownership of Ruthless Records will affect Eazy's seven children. "That's who's really going to suffer from this. We were talking about doing an N.W.A album and giving Eazy's share to his kids."

Dre's words stop suddenly. He's looking off somewhere, palming the back of his neck, perhaps reliving all the years of his life, personal and public: the Wreckin' Cru, N.W.A, his run-ins with the law, Death Row, all the awards and accolades, the offers to produce superstars

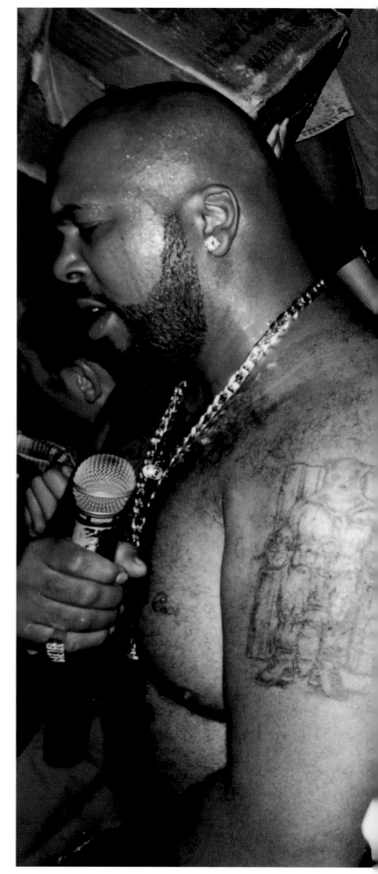

such as Madonna, his and Ice Cube's long-awaited *Helter Skelter* album, Snoop's trial . . .

I pull Dre back into conversation by asking, "Would Death Row exist without you?" His expression becomes blank, then he begins to speak but stops himself and thinks for a moment. "Wherever I am, whatever I do is going to be the bomb shit. And people are going to benefit from it. I dunno, there might be another Dr. Dre out there somewhere." He laughs uneasily.

I ask him about his greatest fear. "I'm not afraid of anything at the moment," he replies. "Actually, I'm afraid of two things: God and the IRS." He laughs again. "That's it. You know, I get butterflies every time a record comes out. I'm, like, I hope people like it. I hope people buy it. But it's never no serious fear."

What matters most to Dr. Dre is the digestion and creation of music: "A lot of times when I'm at home kickin' it, I don't even listen to hip hop," he says. "I listen to all types of music." (He promises Death Row ventures into rock, reggae, and jazz.) Pushing forward in his chair, Dre, who's recently taken up the trumpet, taps his fingers on his left knee excitedly. "My personal opinion is, the '70s is when the best music was made. Some motherfuckers had orchestras! Had string sections and they'd have to sit there and orchestrate a song. And put some vocals to it. So they really got into it. Curtis Mayfield, that motherfucker was bad as shit. Isaac Hayes, Barry White, y'knowhumsayin'? Them brothers was in there doing it."

Out in the crisp air of El Mirage Desert Dry Lake Bed (a grueling 100-mile trek north from Los Angeles) stands the $600,000 video set of "California Love," Tupac's phat first single (co-rapped and produced by Dr. Dre) from *All Eyez on Me*. The video, directed by Hype Williams, is loosely based on the flick *Mad Max*: Helicopters fly overhead, dirt bikes kick up sand, and everyone in the shoot–including Tupac, Dre, comedian/actor Chris Tucker, and a plethora of male and female extras–is wearing black leather shirts, vests, gloves, hats, and pants with metal spikes. Desert dust coats their faces, hands, and arms.

I haven't seen Tupac Shakur since our Rikers Island interview last January. I make my way to his trailer and knock. The door swings open, releasing a powerful gust of chronic smoke. There he is, the big eyes shining brightly, the smile still childlike and broad as an ocean, his exposed muscles–probably due to his 11-month bid–bigger than ever.

As Shakur is whisked away to a TV interview, I ask, "What do you think about this whole East Coast versus West Coast thing?" Tupac smiles that wicked smile and says, "It's gonna get deep."

What is even deeper is the way the word *family* has been mentioned by everyone associated with Death Row, including newcomers like teenage R&B singer Danny Boy and rapper/producer Sam Sneed. In this often cruel and unjust world, it can't be argued enough how important it is to have people who've got your back. To have, as we say, "fam with ya." Shakur's journey–from Harlem and the Bronx to Baltimore to the Bay Area to Los Angeles to Atlanta and back to New York and now back to Los Angeles–has always been about that need for family.

A few weeks later I speak with Shakur via telephone. "The family part, to me–I'm not gonna be corny and be, like, 'Everybody on Death Row love each other,'" he says. "It's not like that. Nobody has beef internally. And if we do, we handle it internally.

"More than a family, Death Row to me is like a machine. The biggest, strongest superpower in the hip hop world. In order to do the things that I gotta do, we gotta have that superpower. Now we gotta expand and show exactly what a superpower is.

"At Death Row I don't have to worry about embarrassing nobody or standing out or doing something they don't want me to do. I'm still Tupac. At Death Row, I got my own shit. I'm independent. But this is the machine that I roll with.

"As for me and Suge, right now–as of today–we're the perfect couple. I can see this is what I've been looking for, managementwise. He rides like I ride. With Suge as my manager, I gotta do less. 'Cause before, niggas wasn't scared of me. So I brought fear to them. Now I don't have to do all that to get respect. 'Cause motherfuckers is scared shitless of Suge. I don't know why, cause Suge's cool. A lot of cowards are trying to make it like Suge's the scourge of the industry. All Suge's doing is riding. Making it so rappers can get what they due."

Back at the video shoot, as another TV crew tapes him, a hyper Tupac spreads out a stack of $100 bills just handed him by Knight, who stands in the background talking on a cellular phone. "This is why I signed to Death Row," says Pac to the cameras, "right here."

Shakur's antics hit me as poignant because–perhaps unwittingly–he's playing right into the hands of people who view rappers as foulmouthed, money-sex-and-violence-crazed lowlifes who are poisoning America's youth. Of course, one of the beauties of the hip hop generation is that we really don't give a fuck what "outsiders" think about us. But in not giving a fuck, in having no agenda but our own selfish needs, are we ultimately fucking all the people (family, real friends, ardent supporters) who see us as representative of dreams so often deferred?

I'm still pondering this a week later at the Los Angeles County Criminal Court Building. The washed-out, gray, nineteen-story structure looks as intimidating as any other courthouse, but this one is notable for its famous defendants: O.J. Simpson, Heidi Fleiss, Michael Jackson. I'm here to witness the *People vs. Calvin Broadus* (a.k.a. Snoop Doggy Dogg) murder trial.

On the ninth floor, in department 110, room no. 9-302, Judge Paul G. Flynn is presiding over jury selection. Some 500 prospective jurors have been interviewed, and 11 have tentatively been agreed upon by the prosecution and defense. While the search for No. 12 continues, my eyes are on Snoop and his codefendant McKinley Lee–the accused triggerman–a dark-skinned young man with a shiny bald head and a thin goatee. In the interviews, Rodney King and O.J. Simpson come up often, as does the issue of race. While Lee pays close attention, especially to questions about potential jurors' views on rap music, Snoop, his permed hair pulled back into a bun, hunches over a legal pad, scribbling, looking up only when his lawyer David Kenner whispers into his ear.

During the lunch break, Snoop leaves the building with his bodyguard and friends (he's free to walk the streets because Knight bailed him out). Meanwhile, Kenner, a short, cock-diesel man with jet black hair, offers that Lee and Snoop acted in self-defense in the fatal shooting of Philip Woldemariam in August 1993. If convicted, both men face life imprisonment.

Kenner, who represents Death Row on both entertainment and criminal matters, insists that "Snoop Doggy Dogg is not on trial here; Calvin Broadus is. When you reach to a performer's interviews or their songs," Kenner says, "and try to extrapolate from that perceptions that you want to draw about the real person, to me it would be no different than saying Arnold Schwarzenegger is a cold-blooded murderer because of his last movie."

That point aside, Kenner expects the prosecution to bring Snoop's lyrics, videos, and interviews into evidence. Several people who have had contact with Snoop over the past three years, including this writer, have been subpoenaed as material witnesses. Just a few days earlier, charges against a third codefendant, Sean Abrams, were dropped. Kenner also asserts that serious questions of missing evidence have yet to be answered.

Returning just before proceedings resume, Snoop, as rawboned as ever in a dark green double-breasted suit, pauses to speak with me. "I'm straight, you know," he says, picking at the strands of hair cupping his chin. "Everybody's praying for me, and I want them to continue to pray for me."

WE CALLED IT DEATH ROW 'CAUSE MOST EVERYBODY HAD BEEN INVOLVED WITH THE LAW. A MAJORITY OF OUR PEOPLE WAS PAROLEES OR INCARCERATED—IT'S NO JOKE.

I ask Snoop if he feels rap music is on trial. His eyes meet mine and narrow. "Yeah, it is. I can't really speak about it, but listen to me, it is."

What about critics who say this trial shows what rap music is all about—violence?

"It's God, giving us obstacles," he replies. "He puts everybody that's successful through obstacles to see if they'll maintain and become successful years down the line. So I'm ready for whatever."

"What do you say to people who look up to you as a hero?"

"Keep God first. Visualize a goal and try to reach it, and if you can't reach it, find something else other than the negative. Because that negative is a long stretch behind the wall—trust me."

There's no ignoring the violence pervading hip hop culture. Particularly when it seems to be reaching up to executive levels. In my interview with Suge Knight, I ask him about the murder in Atlanta of his close friend, Jake Robles. Does he really believe Puffy Combs, the biggest hitmaker on the East Coast, actually had something to do with it? Unnerved by the question, Knight changes the subject, and it isn't brought up again. However, when it's clear the interview is over, he says he has some things he wants to discuss with me.

For the first time that evening, Damu the dog raises up off the red carpet and turns in my direction. "I didn't like them questions you was asking me about the dead," Knight says, anger curling the corners of his mouth. "You mean the questions about Eazy-E?" I ask cautiously.

"Nah, that was my homeboy that was killed down there in Atlanta. I felt you was being disrespectful, and I don't forget things like that," Knight says matter-of-factly, his eyes boring into mine.

As Knight lectures me, the possible seeds of this supposed feud between Knight and Combs come to mind: Tupac Shakur wondering in VIBE last year whether Combs and Biggie Smalls may have known something about his being shot; rumors (strongly denied) that Shakur was raped in jail; Knight publicly dissing Combs—"You don't need no executive producer who's all over your record and in the videos"—at last year's televised *Source* Awards in New York; and finally, the murder of Knight's buddy in Atlanta.

The Atlanta story, according to eyewitnesses, goes a little something like this: SoSoDef Records CEO Jermaine Dupri had a birthday party, which Knight and Combs attended. Later, both showed up at an after-party at the Platinum House. An argument started outside the club, and Knight's friend was killed. According to Combs, Knight turned to him after the shooting and said, "You had to have something to do with this." Given the high profiles of both Knight and Combs, it's ironic that there was barely any mention of the incident in the media.

Interestingly enough, both Knight and Combs are on record denying there's a beef. Knight: "For what? I'm a man. How does that look for me to go and have a beef with a person who's not a threat to me?" Combs: "I'm not a gangsta, and I don't have no rivalry with no person in the industry whatsoever. The whole shit is stupid—tryin' to make an East Coast/West Coast war. East Coast, West Coast, Death Row, Def Jam, or Uptown, I feel nothing but proud for anybody young and black and making money. [Some people] want us to be at each other, at war with each other. Acting like a bunch of ignorant niggas."

But there's no denying that tension's in the air. Some folks say it's the start of a hip hop civil war. I remember Dr. Dre saying, "If it keeps going this way, pretty soon niggas from the East Coast ain't gonna be able to come out here and be safe. And vice versa."

Back in the office, when Knight feels he's gotten his point across, he and Damu turn and head over to his desk. I rise slowly, then exit.

Out in the night air, I sigh hard. This has not been an easy article to deal with. Too many people have warned me about what to say and what not to say, and that, to me, is not what hip hop is about. But then again, it's 1996 and shit is thick for black folks. When a people feel like social, political, or economic outcasts, it gets easier to consider taking one another out—even over the pettiest beefs—in the name of survival. Not even journalists are immune to this logic.

The tragedy here is that two of the most successful young black entrepreneurs ever could possibly end up hurt or dead over God only knows what. As VIBE went to press, there was talk of involving people such as Minister Louis Farrakhan or Ben Chavis in an effort to get both sides to make peace. The future of hip hop may ultimately depend on such a meeting.

How long Death Row Records will live remains to be seen. But like a true player setting his rules for the game, Knight predicts, perhaps not recognizing the double meaning of his words, "Death Row's going to be here forever."

ALL EYEZ

When I was in Los Angeles interviewing the Death Row posse, I was told Tupac Shakur wasn't available to talk. But after Randy "Stretch" Walker was killed, I felt the need to contact Shakur. What I thought would be a five-minute conversation lasted well over an hour. "Lemme get my cigarettes," Shakur said as he got comfortable. He was, as usual, very candid.

Did you move to Death Row for some sort of protection?

Hell, no. There's nobody in the business strong enough to scare me. I'm with Death Row 'cause they not scared either.

When I was in jail, Suge was the only one who used to see me. Nigga used to fly a private plane, all the way to New York, and spend time with me. He got his lawyer to look into all my cases. Suge supported me, whatever I needed. When I got out of jail, he had a private plane for me, a limo, five police officers for security. I said, "I need a house for my moms"; I got a house for my moms.

I promised him, "Suge, I'm gonna make Death Row the biggest label in the whole world. I'm gonna make it bigger than Snoop even made it." Not stepping on Snoop's toes; he did a lot of work. Him, Dogg Pound, Nate Dogg, Dre, all of them—they made Death Row what it is today. I'm gonna take it to the next level.

Is it true your marriage was annulled?

Yeah. I moved too fast. I can only be committed to my work or my wife. I didn't want to hurt her; she's a good person. So we just took it back to where we were before.

I wanna put a rumor to rest. Did something happen to you in prison?

Kill that rumor. That got started either by some guards or by some jealous niggas. I don't have to talk about whether or not I got raped in jail. If I wouldn't lay down on the floor for two niggas with pistols, what the fuck make you think I would bend over for a nigga without weapons? That don't even fit my character.

Do you or Death Row have any beef with Puffy or Biggie?

[Laughs] I don't got no beef with nobody, man. I let the music speak for itself. If you know, you know; if you don't, you don't. Ain't no mystery—niggas know what time it is.

So is this an East Coast/West Coast thing?

It's not like I got a beef with New York or nothing, but I do have problems. And I'm representing the West Side now. There's people disrespecting the West Coast—"It's only gangsta shit, it ain't creative enough, it's fucking up the art form"—even though we made more money for this art form than all those other motherfuckers. The artists now who selling records stole

ON HIM

our style. Listen to 'em—Biggie is a Brooklyn nigga's dream of being West Coast.

You used the word jealousy—

Let's be real. Be real, Kev. Doesn't Biggie sound like me? Is that my style coming out of his mouth? Just New York–tized. That big player shit. He's not no player—I'm the player.

What about all the kids who look up to you and Biggie who don't understand all this?

Regardless of all this stuff—no matter what he say, what I say—Biggie's still my brother. He's black. He's my brother. We just have a conflict of interest. We have a difference of opinion.

How can we stop this disagreement before someone gets killed?

I don't want it to be about violence. I want it to be about money. I told Suge my idea: Bad Boy make a record with all the East Coast niggas. Death Row make a record with all the West Coast niggas. We drop the records on the same day. Whoever sell the most records, that's who the bombest. And then we stop battling. We could do pay-per-views for charity, for the community.

What about Death Row and Bad Boy doing something together?

That's as together as we can get. For money.

What about getting together as black men?

We are together as black men—they over there, we over here. If we really gonna live in peace, we all can't be in the same room. Yellow M&M's don't move with green M&M's. I mean, you don't put M&M's peanuts with M&M's plain. You hear me?

What about this hostility that people are feeding into? Can you and Suge and Puffy and Biggie sit down—

But that's corny. That's just for everybody else—they just wanna hear what the conversation is about. I know my life's not in danger. They shouldn't feel like they gotta worry about me. Puffy wrote me while I was in jail. I wrote him back that I don't got no problems with him. I don't want it to be fighting, I just wanna make my money. You can't tell me I've gotta sit down and hug and kiss niggas to make everybody else feel good. If there was beef, niggas would know.

Your new album is called All Eyez on Me. *Can it be described in a phrase?*

Relentless. It's like, so—uncensored. I do not suggest that children buy this album. There's a lot of cursing. There's a lot of raw game that needs to be discussed in a family moment before you let them listen to it.

What would you suggest parents tell their kids to prepare them for it?

Explain to them that because I'm talking about it doesn't mean that it's okay. This comes from someone who just spent eleven and a half months in a maximum-security jail, got shot five times, and was wrongly convicted of a crime he didn't commit. This is not from a normal person.

Do you feel that you're a leader?

I think so. I think I'm a natural-born leader because I'm a good soldier. I know how to bow down to authority if it's authority that I respect. If Colin Powell was president, I'd follow him.

I wanna get into politics. That's the way for us to overcome a lot of our obstacles. Nothing can stop power or recognize power but power. If Bosnia disrespects America, they gonna go to war. 'Cause America wants its respect. And we sit down after they recognize that they should respect America. Before we can communicate, there has to be mutual respect. And we don't have that.

Where's Tupac gonna be in the year 2000?

I'll be much calmer than I am now.

Why aren't you calm right now?

You know—how would you feel if someone violated you? I was set up. I would rather have been shot straight-up in cold blood—but to be set up? By people who you trusted? That's bad.

Why do you think so many young black men around the country identify with you?

'Cause we all soldiers, unfortunately. Everybody's at war with different things. With ourselves. Some are at war with the establishment. Some of us are at war with our own communities.

What are you at war with?

Different things at different times. My own heart sometimes. There's two niggas inside me. One wants to live in peace, and the other won't die unless he's free.

What about the Tupac who's the son of a Black Panther, and Tupac the rapper?

Tupac the son of the Black Panther, and Tupac the rider. Those are the two people inside of me. My mom and them envisioned this world for us to live in, and strove to make that world. So I was raised off those ideals, to want those.

But in my own life, I saw that that world was impossible to have. It's a world in our head. It's a world we think about at Christmas and Thanksgiving. I had to teach my mother how to live in this world like it is today. She taught me how to live in that world that we have to strive for. And for that I'm forever grateful. She put heaven in my heart. *Kevin Powell*

JUNE 1996

. . . 2Pac deserves credit for avoiding the generic. Mr. Controversy goes twenty-seven tracks deep on *All Eyez on Me,* with a roster of guests—Dr. Dre, Snoop Doggy Dogg, George Clinton, Roger Troutman, Method Man, and Redman, among others—that rivals the cast of *The Towering Inferno* for star power. So why does it all go up in flames? Sounding slapped together, the album degenerates from disposable pleasures like "All Bout U" and "Got My Mind Made Up" to a mish-mash of boring smut ("What's Ya Phone #"), female baiting ("Wonda Why They Call U Bytch"), and routine gangsta life endorsements ("Thug Passion")—all submerged in a sea of played-out samples. Only extra-patient fans will still be bumping this album when Pac *finally* speaks on the events of his recent past. *All Eyez on Me* is not the crime Pac has actually been convicted of, but it's pretty bad. Pass me the cellular, I'm calling the hip hop cops. . . .

Chairman Mao

BULLETS OVER BROOKLYN

On December 16, amid denials of a coastal rap rivalry, gunshots were fired at the trailer that housed Tha Dogg Pound and Snoop Dogg as they were shooting the Pound's video "New York, New York" in Brooklyn. The video, in which Daz and Kurupt take over N.Y.C., finished at that location early but continued filming elsewhere in the city. While the Death Row camp casually dismissed the incident, the bullets remain a mystery to New York's Finest. The video is due later this spring.

I'm glad Suge helped Tupac and all that, but Tupac needs to stop sucking up to him. Fear and respect aren't synonymous, and just 'cause Suge's got 'em scared doesn't

APRIL 1996

mean Tupac will get the respect. Platinum sales run in the blood of Snoop and Dre, no matter who they "ride" with. And I can only hope that some of that blood spills over onto my brother Tupac, because all that Suge and Death Row giveth they can surely taketh away.

Liz Mike
Bryan, TX

I don't think anyone can question the talents of Suge Knight. No matter how you look at it, $100 million in sales is impressive in any business. However, your interview with him left a bad taste in my mouth. Yes, there must be things happening in Suge's life that warrant the high-security measures. But the perpetuation of this "Don't mess with me" image appears very childish and counterproductive: blood red furniture, a trained killer dog named Damu, and a logo on the floor that isn't ever dared to be walked upon? (How about hanging it on the wall?) You're a black male, 30 years old, and a multimillionaire who should be above that corny crap. And it appears to us on the outside like you're overdramatizing your power. Your position already com-

mands respect—why does fear and intimidation have to be added into the equation?

Shindana Crawford
Albany, NY

Tupac must be an idiot to think that record sales determine "the bombest MC." Let's not forget all the records MC Hammer and Vanilla Ice sold, and everyone knows how wack they are. Also, about this battle situation, no problem: I propose Tupac, Snoop, Daz, Kurupt, Sam Sneed, and Dre (I left Rage out because she sounds like she's from the East) bring the noise to a neutral spot somewhere in Chicago and challenge some of the East Coast's finest: KRS-One (who could probably take them out himself), B.I.G., Nas, Redman, Jeru the Damaja, and Q-Tip. Battle it out with no guns, stage shows, naked girls, or gimmicks—just beats and rhymes. Also, to make money, put it on pay-per-view and have call-in voting after every matchup. Then we will see who the real MCs are.

The Coalition to Save
Real Hip Hop
Newark, NJ

Why is it that we as black Americans must resolve conflict through anger and violence? The feud developing between Puffy Combs and Suge is another example of two men who must exercise their egos through male bravado or by threatening to put a gun to someone's head.

It's a shame that two smart entrepreneurs, who've built mega-empires, can't act civil toward one another and must use violence as a means of communication. When does it all end? Black-on-black crime, Bloods versus Crips, East Coast versus West Coast? When will blacks learn that economic power comes from sticking together, loving each other, and helping each other along? We are the only group of people that hasn't learned this concept. The Koreans, Jews, and Italians know how to play this game. Blacks, on the other hand, are still water boys fetching water for the man.

Name Withheld
pl27frs@aol.com

Death Row and Suge Knight are a perfect example of why we as black people will never be united. Suge's violent scare tactics, Tupac's paranoia, and Dre's deep denial show Death Row for what it really is—a bunch of gangstas who can't conduct business on a professional level. They're just a bunch of West Coast G's wishing they were New York players! And Tupac was bought and paid for like a modern-day slave. Kunta-Tupac better hope Master Suge don't cut off his foot, because evidently he already cut off Pac's balls.

Marcia Best
Richmond Hill, NY

Tupac Shakur is a household name who gets much respect

from me. He has proven to be a very intelligent black man who knows what he wants out of life. I really would love to see him become a political leader, because I feel he would represent Africans here in white America. Blacks need someone who isn't scared of anything or anyone who walks the earth, and Tupac has such power that anyone who listens to his music deeply with an open mind can feel it. He's definitely the Malcolm X of the 1990s.

Lena R.
Detroit, MI

I am a 64-year-old grandmother who (with some reservations) loves and supports hip hop culture and its artists. The enmity between East and West Coast rappers

MAY 1996

rang a bell for me. So I have advice for this generation: The civil rights and Black Power movements from the '60s taught me that young men need to move very cautiously to avoid being drawn or pushed into a war against each other. Brothers, keep your wits about you. Do not be provoked into violence. Don't do any more *New York Times Magazine* cover stories about your status and power: It's a setup. I've seen this scenario before. It sounds like paranoia, but believe me, it's reality.

Florence Tate
Washington, DC

RUNNIN' MATES

The East Coast–West Coast rivalry gets crazier daily, but Mergela Records has brought the two main combatants together—at least on wax. In early January, the infant indie label released a "new" track featuring the Notorious B.I.G., Tupac Shakur, and the late Randy "Stretch" Walker to urban radio stations across the country.

The Easy Mo Bee–produced song, "Runnin'," was recorded back in August 1994 when Biggie, Tupac, and Stretch (Shakur's former aide-de-camp who was murdered last November) were still boys. Considering the bad blood that currently exists between the two stars, it's no surprise that neither had much to say about the song, which is included on the Million Man March–inspired compilation *One Million Strong.* Tupac issued an official "no comment" through a spokesperson, while Easy Mo Bee's lawyer wanted assurance that his client would not be asked about the East-West feud. As for Biggie, he would only say, "I support any brother who wants to move in the direction of more responsibility to our unity. We're all trying to get paid. Anything else is just bullshit."

David Bry

Faith's motives and actions have been under constant scrutiny since August 4, 1994—the day she and Biggie wedded. "People assumed I was just some cute girl that was using him," she says with a sarcastic laugh. "Hello? I was already doin' my thing."

The honeymoon was over soon after they married. Biggie had to go on the road, while Faith stayed in Brooklyn, working hard on her album. "Not seeing him at all," she admits, "was terrible." After her album was done, Biggie started working with his protégés Junior M.A.F.I.A. "A few months after our anniversary, it seemed like he was getting caught up in all that Big Poppa stuff. But I couldn't see myself being without him. He was real . . . real . . ." She searches for the right word. "Real."

It wasn't until January—a month before *Eyez* was released—that Faith says Death Row (then entangled in a ridiculous East-West rivalry with Bad Boy) sent a letter requesting clearance for her to sing on the record. But the two labels could not reach an agreement.

"I heard the rumors," she says, "and thought, Tupac's bananas. But there's so much garbage now, I don't even pay it no mind." For the record, Faith says she never slept with Tupac. She says she hasn't spoken to him since she was in L.A. "And if I saw him," she says quietly, "I don't know what I would do or say."

Faith's ordeal is a clear reflection of the misogyny that continues to thrive in hip hop. Tupac, in a tired effort to regain his player role, attacks Biggie's wife. And like Anita

FAITH. FULLY.

Faith Evans is a talented singer/songwriter with a successful album, a beautiful face, and a sassy baby daughter— so how come all everyone wants to talk about are the Notorious B.I.G. and Tupac? *By Karen R. Good*

Which is not the word she searches for when speaking of Tupac Shakur. Faith says she met Tupac in October 1995, a couple of days after his release from New York's Clinton Correctional Facility. She was in Los Angeles, writing for an R&B group called Tha Truth while Shakur was recording *All Eyez on Me* for Death Row Records. "He was mad cool," Faith says with a hint of surprise. "I saw him at a couple of parties, and we was chillin', havin' drinks, him and my friends. And I knew Biggie always said he had mad love for Tupac." (At least he did before Shakur insinuated that Biggie was somehow involved in the attempt on his life in November 1994.)

According to Faith, Shakur asked her to work on *All Eyez*, and she agreed, pending Bad Boy's okay. Before heading back to New York, she recorded a rough vocal for Pac. Next thing Faith knew, people were telling her she was on Shakur's new album, on a track called "Wonda Why They Call U Bytch" (though according to Death Row, the vocalist is Jewell).

Hill and Robin Givens, Faith is portrayed in terms that are repeatedly used to devalue black womanhood. In her book *Killing Rage*, bell hooks writes, "Black women are represented as liars, as uppity, disobedient, disloyal, and out of control."

Actually, Faith remains poised and centered. "I know I'm a good person," she says with a slight neck roll. "I don't even have to pay extra close attention to how I deal with stuff, 'cause I know God ain't gonna let nothing happen to me that's not meant for something to be learned behind it." You can tell, too, that the symphony of blues that threatened to consume her life is lifting, the blurriness slowly coming into focus.

Tucked demurely on the back of Faith's right shoulder is a new tattoo, a crucifix. "I got it in L.A., before all this extra drama," she says, throwing her shoulder toward me to show it off. "I was going through a lot with Biggie and just mad other stuff in my life. So I got my cross," she testifies, " 'cause the cross I got to bear."

STRAIGHT OFFA

JUNE 1996

Another California earthquake ripped through the hip hop nation, and once again its epicenter was Death Row Records. Dr. Dre, cofounder of the four-year-old company and the creative force behind its $125 million success, has reportedly left to form his own label. At press time, none of the parties involved would comment on Dre's departure, but sources told VIBE it's just a matter of time before he signs with Interscope and announces his new plans.

Since January, rumors of Dre leaving Death Row ricocheted through the industry like stray bullets. The alleged reasons were myriad: Death Row cofounder and CEO Suge Knight was upset that Dre didn't appear on *Saturday Night Live* with Tupac in February or show up at Snoop Doggy Dogg's murder trial; that Dre wanted to introduce rock, reggae, and jazz into Death Row's musical mix while Knight wanted to stick to hip hop and R&B; and that Dre was leaving to hook up with Def Jam's Russell Simmons. Neither Death Row nor Interscope would comment.

Simmons, however, wanted to clarify his role in the drama. "The rumors of me signing Dre are false," he says. "I'd pay any amount of money to be in business with him, but we've had no discussion."

Joseph V. Tirella

DEATH ROW

. . . Tupac Shakur was sentenced in April to 120 days in jail for failing to serve 15 days on a California freeway cleanup crew as part of his probation for a 1994 assault and battery conviction. He has until June 7 to turn himself in. . . .

Questions have constantly been raised to whether or not Tupac Shakur has matured after his incarceration several months ago. *VIBEonline* conducted an exclusive interview with Tupac to find what really is making him tick, and what exactly has him ticked off.

What motivates you?

Poverty, needs, wants, pain. Now I'm dealing with a more military type of philosophy—to mix the street life with respected, known, and proven military philosophy. So when I'm rapping and talking that hardcore shit, at least it'll be from a military mind-set.

What about your father—do you have any relationship with him?

I thought my father was dead all my life. After I got shot, I looked up and there was this nigga that looked just like me. And he was my father; that's when I found out. We still didn't take no blood test but the nigga looked just like me and the other nigga's dead, so now I feel that I'm past the father stage. I do want to know him and I do know him.

We did talk and he did visit and help me when I was locked down, but I'm past that. What I want to do is form a society in which we can raise ourselves; so we can become our own father figures and the big homies can become their father figures, and then you grow up, then it's your turn to be a father figure to another young brother. That's where I want to start. Nine times out of ten, though, we would want them to be there, they can't be depended on to be there. Now, some of the mothers can't be there because they doing their thing [working]. I can't blame them, they gotta do what they gotta do. So I think the youth should raise themselves since they got lofty ideas about what's theirs and their rights, what they should deserve. Since you can't whup their asses, these motherfuckers should get out and work at fifteen. I want to be a part of the generation that builds the groundwork for us to raise each other.

In one of your VIBE interviews, you mentioned an organization that you were starting with Mike Tyson. What happened with that?

Now I'm doing it with Death Row. I was going to do it myself and I found out when I was about to be sentenced to jail that there was a spot called "A Place Called Home." I was about to be sent to jail for an old gun case that I had. The judge was like "You can tell your side of who you are" and the prosecutor gave this big fat envelope of every time I got arrested and all this stuff that made me look like a crazed animal.

We got someone who didn't work for us to write my life's story, talking about everybody in my family and the people that I helped. This lady from the community center wrote as well. We were planning already to do this big concert with me and my homeboys to raise money to have a center in North Central where we can have the "at risk" kids come to a spot that they can call home—where they can get guidance, tutoring, love, nurturing. We're going to do a spot like that.

So instead of it just being a program with me and Tyson like I planned it, 'cause it's me sitting in the penitentiary thinking, is

INSIDE THE MIND OF SHAKUR

now moved into this program called "A Place Called Everybody Home" that I'm working closely with. There's also a program called "Celebrity Youth League," with me, Hammer, Suge, and all of these sports figures each going to sponsor a youth group all year in football, baseball, and basketball. We sponsor the team, buy the uniforms, hire the coach, and start our own Little League.

How do you relax from all this that you're doing?

There's three ways: shopping, driving down Sunset with the top down on any car, and being with my homeboys. Not necessarily the older homies but the younger ones. Vibing off of what they're talking about and what's going on, and dropping whatever I have to drop to them. Then it's not like I'm doing this shit in vain.

Do you still keep in touch with old friends?

On the whole, I don't have any friends. Friends come and go; I've lost my trust factor. I believe I have people who *think* they're my friends. And I believe that there are people probably in their heart who are friendly toward me or are friends to me. But they're not my friends, because what I learned is that fear is stronger than love. So soon as somebody scarier comes along, they won't be my friend anymore. I learned that on the floor at Times Square—so I don't have friends, I have family. You're either my all-the-way family or just somebody on the outside.

Are you tight with your family?

Yeah, we took it back to the old school. We got the head of the family, we listen to the rules and regulations, order and organization. Now we're a living, breathing family, when before we were a dying, dysfunctional family. We still got problems but now we're learning how to deal with it.

What religion are you?

I'm the religion that to me is the realest religion there is. I try to pray to God every night unless I pass out. I learned this in jail. I talked to every God [member of the Five Percent Nation] there was in jail. I think that if you take one of the "O's" out of "Good" it's "God," if

WHEN PEOPLE ASK SUGE IF HE'S BEEFING WITH BAD BOY AND PUFFY, HE'S SAYS THAT'S LIKE GOING TO THE PLAYGROUND TO PICK ON LITTLE KIDS.

you add a "D" to "Evil," it's the "Devil." I think some cool motherfucker sat down a long time ago and said, Let's figure out a way to control motherfuckers. That's what they came up with—the Bible. 'Cause if God wrote the Bible, I'm sure there would have been a revised copy by now. 'Cause a lot of shit has changed. I've been looking for this revised copy—I still see that same old copy that we had from then. I'm not disrespecting anyone's religion, please forgive me if it comes off that way, I'm just stating my opinion.

The Bible tells us that all these people did this because they suffered so much, that's what makes them special people. I got shot five times and I got crucified in the media. And I walked through with the thorns on, and I had shit thrown on me, and I had the word thief at the top; I told that nigga, "I'll be back for you. Trust me, it's not supposed to be going down, I'll be back." I'm not saying I'm Jesus, but I'm saying we go through that type of thing every day. We don't part the Red Sea, but we walk through the 'hood without getting shot. We don't turn water to wine, but we turn dope fiends and dope heads into productive citizens of society. We turn words into money—what greater gift can there be? So I believe God blesses us, I believe God blesses those that hustle. Those that use their minds and those that overall are righteous. I believe that everything you do bad comes back to you. So everything that I do that's bad, I'm going to suffer for it. But in my heart, I believe what I'm doing in my heart is right. So I feel like I'm going to heaven.

I think heaven is just when you sleep, you sleep with a good conscience—you don't have nightmares. Hell is when you sleep, the last thing you see is all the fucked-up things you did in your life and you just see it over and over again, 'cause you don't burn. If that's the case, it's hell on earth, 'cause bullets burn. There's people that got burned in fires, does that mean they went to hell already? All that is here. What do you got there that we ain't seen here? What, we're gonna walk around aimlessly like zombies? That's here! You ain't been on the streets lately? Heaven now, look! [He gestures to his plush apartment.] We're sitting up here in the living room, big-screen TV—this is heaven, for the moment. Hell is jail—I seen that one. Trust me, this is what's real. And all that other shit is to control you.

If the churches took half the money that they was making and gave it back to the community, we'd be all right. If they took half the buildings that they use to "praise God" and gave it to motherfuckers who need God, we'd be all right. Have you seen some of these got-damn churches lately? There's one's that take up the whole block in New York. There's homeless people out here. Why ain't God lettin' them stay there? Why these niggas got gold ceilings and shit? Why God need gold ceilings to talk to me? Why does God need colored windows to talk to me? Why God can't come where I'm at where he sent me? If God wanted to talk to me in a pretty spot like that, why the hell he send me here then? That makes ghetto kids not believe in God. *Why?*

So that's wrong religion—I believe in God, I believe God puts us wherever we want to be at. That didn't make sense that God would put us in the ghetto. That means he wants us to work hard to get up out of here. That means he's testing us even more. That makes sense that if you're good in your heart, you're closer to God, but if you're evil, then you're closer to the devil; that makes sense! I see that everyday all that other spooky shit, don't make sense. I don't even believe, I'm not dissin' them, but I don't believe in the brothers, I've been in jail with 'em and having conversations with brothers; "I'm God, I'm God." You God, open the gate for me. You know how far the sun is and how far the moon is, how the hell do I pop this fuckin' gate? And get me free and up outta here. Then I'll be a Five Percenter for life.

What type of woman would it take to settle you down?

A very, very strong woman. One who's more in love with me because I could be more in love with her than she is. Every time I fall

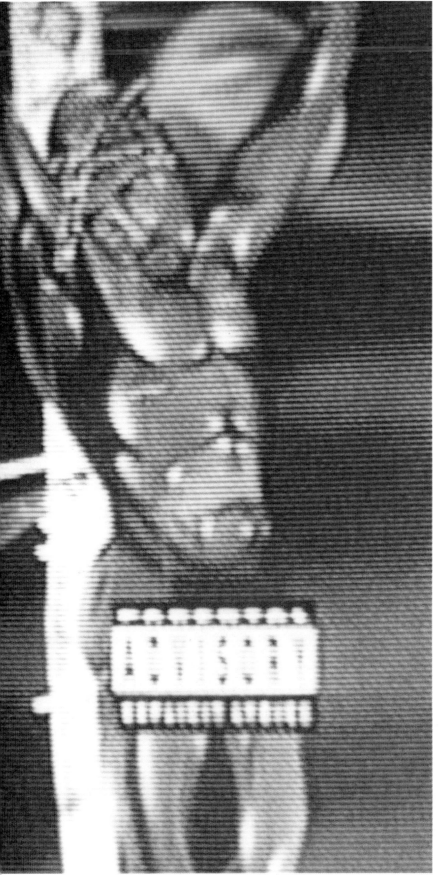

in love with a woman, I don't fall in love with the woman she is, I fall in love with the woman she could be. I haven't found a woman yet that has met my standards. And I'm sure I don't fit up to everyone's standards. But I haven't found one yet, but I found one that I think has the potential to be the rawest woman in the world.

I feel like it's natural for a man, especially being black, to feel like he's the king and he's looking for his queen. That's where I'm at right now. You can't be a king until you've made yourself, until you've done something. And I've accomplished my goals that made me a man. Now I set out goals to make me a king. Not a king of anyone else but me. Nobody else is under my rule but me. I made myself into a king, now I need a queen to be happy so I can be a teacher and a father. I can't be that until I find a queen—so I'm stuck in limbo.

A lot of your East Coast fans feel like your new allegiance to the West Coast is a disloyalty to the East.

That's so much nonsense. Poppycock! (He laughs.) It's not a new allegiance to the West Coast, I've been on the West Coast all this time. Some people, not all, some people on the East Coast are on their dicks so hard, they never heard me say that I'm living on the West Coast. It's just by me keeping it real, I always said where I come from. I always gave New York their props. On *Me Against the World,* I took a whole song to give it up. So now on the next album, when I wanna give it up, for my home, where I'm at, everybody got a problem. Why don't they have a problem with Biggie saying "Brooklyn in the house" every fucking show he do? They just did a Sprite commercial with "The Bridge" and KRS, why isn't it hip hop when I do it?

Everybody else can have a beef within the music, talk about differences and it's OK. It's music, it's hip hop, it's groundbreaking. When I do it, it's war. That's all I'm doing. All I'm doing is saying that I'm tired of you talking about where you're from. If that's what we're gonna do now. We was doing it like hip hop was one nation. I have proof to say what I was doing—I've done more for the East Coast than the East Coast did. I put more guns in East Coast niggas' hands than East Coast niggas did when they came out here. I put them niggas on to more weed gates and weed spots and safe havens and safe spots than the East Coast did. I put more rappers on than they did. I gave Biggie his first shows! I was that bridge that niggas used to walk on to get over here. I explained it, I was the one that told you. I'm why all these niggas are running around with a gangbanger on their payroll now.

Is there still a beef going on between you and Biggie?

There was never a beef, only a difference of opinion. My homeboy Suge gave me the best advice that I could ever get from anybody. When people ask him if he's beefing with Bad Boy and with Puffy, he's says it's like me going to the playground to pick on little kids. That's like me being mad at my little brother 'cause he's getting cash now. I'm not mad at that, I'm just mad at my little brother when he don't respect me. And when you don't respect me, I'ma spank that ass. I don't give a fuck how rich you got on the block, I'm your big brother. I'ma break your big ass down. That's my only point.

I feel as though he got out of hand. He got seduced by the power—not because he's an evil person, but because money is evil if it's not handled right. If you lose your composure, you could do anything. Fear got stronger than love and niggas did things that they weren't really supposed to do. They know in their hearts that's why they're in hell now. They can't sleep. That's why they're telling all the reporters and all the people "Why they doing this? They fucking up hip hop, blah, blah, blah."'Cause they in hell. They can't make money, they can't go anywhere, they can't look at themselves, 'cause they know the prodigal son has returned. I'm alive; the ghost is walking around.

Now, everybody who thinks that I disrespected, I love my East Coast fans. I'm from there. I'm eating New York pizza, I drive New York jeeps, but I'm saying let's keep it real for a second. If you're half the lover of music that you are, go back and study. Study how "Party and Bullshit" was me before I met Biggie. You don't hear my style in his raps. Study how after I met Biggie, *Ready to Die* comes out and his whole style changes. Study why I would be mad when half of the major New York rappers or their managers, or their agents, or their somebody was there when I got shot—and nobody couldn't give me no information. Just study that. Study how when Wu-Tang got their chain snatched at six-six-deuce, I not only found who did it but gave them the message that if they wanted to see the niggas that did it, they could see them. Man to man, just you and them—no guns, no nothing if you feel like that. That's all I ask for. If you're going to act like a gangster or a G or a king of New York, I'ma expect that. And when you don't come through, then I'm going to want to crush your empire. And that's what it's time for.

AUGUST 1996

"You won't hear about me doing anything illegal."
—Tupac Shakur, to an L.A. County judge after pleading guilty to a weapons possession charge (he also promised to organize a benefit show for underprivileged kids)

WEST COAST

Puffy a No-show at East-West Rap Summit. *By OJ Lima*

East Coast meets West Coast in the City of Brotherly Love—that was the idea, anyway. In the spirit of the Million Man March, Dr. Ben Chavis of the National African American Leadership Summit and promoters Paperboy Entertainment tried, among other things, to get Death Row Records CEO Suge Knight and Bad Boy Entertainment CEO Puffy Combs together in mid-May to discuss their differences at the first National Hip Hop and Rap Summit in Philadelphia.

Only things didn't go quite as planned: While Knight attended, he left early; and Combs—who was one of the event's supporters—never showed. He later told New York's Hot 97 FM that he was busy taking care of his son. (When reached at his office, Combs had no further comment on his absence.)

Knight, for his part, spoke to reporters on topics ranging from Dr. Dre's departure from Death Row to hip hop watchdog C. DeLores Tucker, but grew slightly agitated when queried on Combs. "There's nothing between Death Row and Bad Boy, or me and Puffy," he said. "Death Row sells volume—so how could Puffy be a threat to me, or Bad Boy be a threat to Death Row? Right now no black person owns their own groups and masters but me—but I wish someone else did so I could have some competition."

IN THE HOUSE

VIBE: *There's this East Coast–West Coast thing going on between Puffy and Suge. What do you feel about that?*

Clive Davis: Whatever isolated rivalry that's going on is not generational. Music is a competitive industry. And like the film industry, you end up knowing your competitors. When I was head of Columbia, of course I knew [Atlantic Records founder] Ahmet Ertegun, [Warner Bros. chairman] Mo Ostin, and [Motown founder] Berry Gordy. You don't have the situation to yourself. So you compete. So if there is—and I don't know the details—a rivalry between two labels, I don't think it speaks for this generation any more than [former Walt Disney Studios chairman] Jeffrey Katzenberg feuding with [Walt Disney Company chairman] Michael Eisner speaks for another.

VIBE: *You hear stories about Suge and Tupac pulling guns on Puffy and Biggie or whatever . . .*

If any of that is taking place, it has nothing to do with the state of the record industry, nor should it be a categorization of what it is to compete in the '90s. That would be horrifying.

I think the story about the Rap Summit explains one of the reasons why some MCs and hip hop listeners believe the West Coast doesn't have any real love for the music. Suge Knight said, "Death Row sells volume—so how could Puffy be a threat to me?" Easy—by making music that fans can feel. Should we be expected to compromise the art form and the evolution of hip hop for money?

Aamir El Amin
Philadelphia, PA

What the hell is wrong with Puffy Combs? He's always talking about how he'd like to resolve his differences with Suge Knight—even going as far as taking out a full-page ad in your magazine to voice his concern about the issue—but when it's time for him to sit down and talk to Suge man-to-man, he's a no-show! Puffy is really living up to his name—a puff of empty hot air.

Kessa Cockrell
Ethelsville, AL

103

STAYING

VIBE: *How do you feel about this East Coast–West Coast thing? And tell me what it was like five or six years ago.*

Chuck D: Back in '88 when we did the Bring the Noise tour with Stetsasonic and EPMD, we asked Ice to come along with it, we asked the Geto Boys, we put Too Short down, MC Hammer. We had this big crew of different MCs from different parts of the country basically saying, "Yo, man, look, we just happy, we out here playin'. We playin' together. It's about the public. It's about servin' 'em." That's how that East-West shit was knocked down real quick.

Ice-T: I think there's drama now for two reasons. One, Cube and them just got an attitude. I don't know what they're tryin' to do. They're, like, "Come on, we've been kissin' New York's ass for a long time and yet people are still not givin' up the love that we give them when they come out here." Then there's the real beef. Tupac got real beef with Biggie. I just did a show with Tupac last night, [Fox's] *Saturday Night Special*. I told them niggas, I told them straight up, "I'm not with that East Coast–West Coast shit. I got too much love in New York. Fuck that."

VIBE: *And what did they say to that?*

Ice-T: Well, Tupac really believes Biggie and them shot him. I don't know, I wasn't there. But if somebody thinks somebody shot them, it's on for life.

Chuck D: No question.

Ice-T: I don't know what to say about that, but that beef they got, that's real, that's not East Coast–West Coast shit.

Chuck D: That's between those two camps right there.

VIBE: *Why is it happening? Isn't part of it about straight competition to sell records?*

Ice-T: Here's a good example. I was on the radio the other night, and they was asking me, "Well, why can't brothers get along, why can't y'all just be down with each other?" And I was on 92 the Beat. I said, "Why can't I say Power 106 on this station?" Why can't VIBE talk positively about *The Source?* Because it's competition. Right now rap is business, millions of dollars are exchanging hands.

Chuck D: It's business, but you gotta at least tell motherfuckers, "Don't be backing up onto the Tec," you know what I'm saying? We have to remember that this is the shit that made us. We need to take care of it.

Ice-T: When I started rhyming, I really didn't take it seriously. As I started coming up, I'm, like, "Wow, people really pay attention to what I'm saying," you know? I didn't realize this was about power. *Danyel Smith*

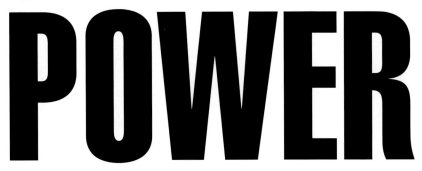

POWER

EAST COAST STRIKES BACK

The tradition of hip hop response records is alive and well. This time Tragedy, Capone, Noreaga, and Mobb Deep have answered Tha Dogg Pound's provocative "New York, New York" with the equally incendiary "L.A., L.A." The video, which began running in late April, features the East Coast rappers kidnapping and torturing a faux Daz and Kurupt. In the end Daz is suffocated with an "I Love NY" bag, and his body gets thrown off the 59th Street Bridge. "It's not like we're trying to shit on L.A.," says Tragedy, "but we didn't want the East being disrespected."

STAKES IS HIGH

Puffy and Biggie Break Their Silence on Tupac, Death Row, and All the East-West Friction. A Tale of Bad Boys and Bad Men.
By The Blackspot

Now, we can settle this like we got some class, or we can get into some gangster shit.
—Max Julien as Goldie in *The Mack*

It's hard to believe that someone who has seen so much could have such young eyes. But the eyes of Sean "Puffy" Combs, bright, brown, and alert, reflect the stubborn innocence of childhood. His voice, however, tells another story. Sitting inside the control room of Daddy's House Studios in midtown Manhattan, dressed in an Orlando Magic jersey and linen slacks, Puffy speaks in low, measured tones, almost whispering.

"I'm hurt a little bit spiritually by all the negativity, by this whole Death Row–Bad Boy shit," says Puffy, president of Bad Boy Entertainment, one of the most powerful creative forces in black music today. And these days, one of the most tormented. "I'm hurt that out of all my accomplishments, it's like I'm always getting my most fame from negative drama. It's not like the young man that was in the industry for six years, won the ASCAP Songwriter of the Year, and every record he put out went at least gold. . . . All that gets overshadowed. How it got to this point, I really don't know. I'm still trying to figure it out."

So is everyone else. What's clear is that a series of incidents—Tupac Shakur catching bullets at a New York studio in November '94, a close friend of Death Row CEO Suge Knight being killed at an Atlanta party in September '95, the Notorious B.I.G. and Tupac facing off after the *Soul Train* Music Awards in L.A. this past March—have led to much finger-pointing and confusion. People with little or no connection to Death Row or Bad Boy are choosing up sides. From the Atlantic to the Pacific, hip hop heads are proclaiming their "California Love" or exclaiming that "the East is in the house" with the loyalty of newly initiated gang members. As Dr. Dre put it, "Pretty soon, niggas from the East Coast ain't gonna be able to come out here and be safe. And vice versa."

Meanwhile, the two camps that have the power to put an end to it all have yet to work out their differences. Moreover, Suge Knight's Death Row camp, while publicly claiming there is no beef, has continued to aggravate the situation: first, by making snide public comments about the Bad Boy family, and second, by releasing product that makes the old Dre vs. Eazy conflict look tame. The intro to the video for the Tupac/Snoop Doggy Dogg song "2 of Americaz Most Wanted" features two characters named Pig and Buff who are accused of setting up Tupac and are then confronted in their office. And the now infamous B-side, "Hit 'Em Up," finds Tupac, in a fit of rage, telling Biggie, "I fucked your bitch, you fat motherfucker," and

SEPTEMBER 1996

then threatening to wipe out all of Bad Boy's staff and affiliates.

While the records fly off the shelves and the streets get hotter, Puffy and Big have remained largely silent. Both say they've been reluctant to discuss the drama because the media and the public have blown it out of proportion. At press time, there were rumors festering that Puffy—who was briefly hospitalized June 30 for a cut arm—had tried to commit suicide, causing many to wonder if the pressure had become too much. Determined to put an end to all the gossip, Puffy and Big have decided to tell their side.

Why would I set a nigga up to get shot?" says Puffy. "If I'ma set a nigga up, which I would never do, I ain't gonna be in the country. I'ma be in Bolivia somewhere." Once again, Puffy is answering accusations that he had something to do with Shakur's shooting at New York's Quad Recording Studio, the event that sowed the seeds of Tupac's beef with the East.

In April 1995, Tupac told VIBE that moments after he was ambushed and shot in the building's lobby, he took the elevator up to the studio, where he saw about forty people, including Biggie and Puffy. "Nobody approached me. I noticed that nobody would look at me," said Tupac, suggesting that the people in the room knew he was going to be shot. In "Hit 'Em Up," Tupac does more than suggest, rapping, "Who shot me? But ya punks didn't finish / Now you're about to feel the wrath of a menace."

I AIN'T A GANGSTER, SAYS PUFFY, SO WHY Y'ALL GONNA TELL ME TO START ACTING LIKE A GANGSTER?

But Puffy says Tupac's barking up the wrong tree: "He ain't mad at the niggas that shot him; he knows where they're at. He knows who shot him. If you ask him, he knows, and everybody in the street knows, and he's not stepping to them, because he knows that he's not gonna get away with that shit. To me, that's some real sucker shit. Be mad at everybody, man; don't be using niggas as scapegoats. We know that he's a nice guy from New York. All shit aside, Tupac is a nice, good-hearted guy."

Taking a break from recording a new joint for his upcoming album, *Life After Death,* Big sinks into the studio's sofa in a blue Sergio Tacchini running suit that swishes with his every movement. He is visibly bothered by the lingering accusations. "I'm still thinking this nigga's my man," says Big, who first met Tupac in 1993 during the shooting of John Singleton's *Poetic Justice.* "This shit's just got to be talk, that's all I kept saying to myself. I can't believe he would think that I would shit on him like that."

He recalls that on the movie set, Tupac kept playing Big's first single, "Party and Bullshit." Flattered, he met Tupac at his home in L.A., where the two hung out, puffed lah, and chilled. "I always thought it to be like a Gemini thing," he says. "We just clicked off the top and were cool ever since." Despite all the talk, Big claims he remained loyal to his partner in rhyme through thick and thin. "Honestly, I didn't have no problem with the nigga," Big says. "There's shit that muthafuckas don't sho. I saw the situations and how shit was going, and tried to school the nigga. I was there when he bought his first Rolex, but I wasn't in the position to be rolling like that. I think Tupac felt more comfortable with the dudes he was hanging with because they had just as much money as him.

"He can't front on me," says Big. "As much as he may come off as some Biggie hater, he knows. He knows when all that shit was going down, I was schooling a nigga to certain things, me and [Live Squad rapper] Stretch—God bless the grave. But he chose to do the things he wanted to do. There wasn't nothing I could do, but it wasn't like he wasn't my man."

While Tupac was taking shots at Biggie—claiming he'd bit his "player" style and sound—Suge was cooking up his own beef with Bad Boy. At the *Source* Awards in August 1995, Suge made the now legendary announcement, "If you don't want the owner of your label on your album or in your video or on your tour, come sign with Death Row." Obviously directed at Puffy's high-profile role in his artists' careers, the remark came as a shock. "I couldn't believe what he said," Puffy recalls. "I thought we was boys." All the same, when it came time for Puffy to present an award, he said a few words about East-West unity and made a point of hugging the recipient, Death Row artist Snoop Doggy Dogg.

Nonetheless, Suge's words spread like flu germs, reigniting ancient East-West hostilities. It was in this increasingly tense atmosphere that Big and Junior M.A.F.I.A.'s clique reached Atlanta for Jermaine Dupri's birthday party last September. During the after-party at a club called Platinum House, Suge Knight's close friend Jake Robles was shot. He died at the hospital a week later. Published reports said that some witnesses claimed a member of Puffy's entourage was responsible.

At the mention of the incident, Puffy sucks his teeth in frustration. "Here's what happened," he says. "I went to Atlanta with my son. At the same time, there wasn't really no drama. I didn't even have bodyguards, so that's a lie that I did. I left the club, and I'm waiting for my limo, talking to girls. I don't see [Suge] go into the club; we don't make any contact or nothing like that. He gets into a beef in the club with some niggas. I knew the majority of the club, but I don't know who he got into the beef with, what it was over, or nothing like that. All I heard is that he took beef at the bar. I see people coming out. I see a lot of people that I know, I see him, and I see everybody yelling and screaming and shit. I get out the limo and I go to him, like, 'What's up, you all right?' I'm trying to see if I can help. That's my muthafuckin' problem," Puffy says, pounding his fist into his palm in frustration. "I'm always trying to see if I can help somebody.

"Anyway, I get out facing him, and I'm, like, 'What's going on, what's the problem?' Then I hear shots ringing out, and we turn around and someone's standing right behind me. His man—God bless the dead—gets shot, and he's on the floor. My back was turned; I could've got shot, and he could've got shot. But right then he was, like, 'I think you had something to do with this.' I'm, like, 'What are you talking about? I was standing right here with you!' I really felt sorry for him, in the sense that if he felt that way, he was showing me his insecurity."

After the Atlanta shooting, people on both coasts began speculating. Would there be retribution? All-out war? According to a *New York Times Magazine* cover story, Puffy sent Louis Farrakhan's son, Mustafa, to talk with Suge. Puffy says he did not send Mustafa but did tell him, "If there's anything you can do to put an end to this bullshit, I'm with it." The *Times* reported that Suge refused to meet with Mustafa. Suge has since declined to speak about his friend's murder.

Less than two weeks later, when it came time for the "How Can I Be Down?" rap conference in Miami, the heat was on. Suge, who has never concealed his past affiliations with L.A.'s notorious Bloods, was rumored to be coming with an army. Puffy was said to be bringing a mass of New York drug lords and thugs. When the conference came and Puffy did not attend, *Billboard* reported that it was due to threats from Death Row.

On December 16, 1995, it became apparent that the trouble was spilling into the streets. In Red Hook, Brooklyn, shots were fired at the trailer where Death Row artists Tha Dogg Pound were making a video for "New York, New York"—which features Godzilla-size West Coasters stomping on the Big Apple. No one was hurt, but the message was clear. Then came "L.A., L.A.," an answer record from New York MC's Tragedy, Capone, Noreaga, and Mobb Deep. That video featured stand-ins for Tha Dogg Pound's Daz and Kurupt being kidnapped, tortured, and tossed off the 59th Street Bridge.

By this time, the rumor mill had kicked into overdrive. The latest story was that Tupac was boning Biggie's wife, Faith Evans, and Suge was getting with Puffy's ex, Misa Hylton. Death Row allegedly printed up a magazine ad featuring Misa and Suge holding Puffy's two-year-old son, with a caption reading "The East Coast can't even take care of their own." The ad—which was discussed on New York's Hot 97 by resident gossip Wendy Williams—never ran anywhere, but reps were tarnished nonetheless. Death Row now denies that such an ad ever existed. Puffy says he didn't know about any ad. Misa says, "I don't do interviews."

Meanwhile, Tupac kept rumors about himself and Faith alive with vague comments in interviews like "You know I don't kiss and tell." But in "Hit 'Em Up," released this May, he does just that, telling Biggie, "You claim to be a player, but I fucked your wife." (Faith, for her part, denies ever sleeping with Tupac.)

When talk turns to his estranged wife, Biggie shrugs his shoulders and pulls on a blunt. "If the muthafucka really did fuck Fay, that's foul how he's just blowin' her like that," he says. "Never once did he say that Fay did some foul shit to him. If honey was to give you the pussy, why would you disrespect her like that? If you had beef with me, and you're like, 'Boom, I'ma fuck his wife,' would you be so harsh on her? Like you got beef with her? That shit doesn't make sense. That's why I don't believe it."

What was still mostly talk and propaganda took a turn for the ugly at the *Soul Train* Awards this past March. When Biggie accepted his award and bigged-up Brooklyn, the crowd hissed. But the real drama came after the show, when Tupac and Biggie came face to face for the first time since Pac's shooting more than two years before. "That was the first time I really looked into his face," says Big. "I looked into his eyes and I was, like, yo, this nigga is really buggin' the fuck out."

The following week's *Hollywood Reporter* quoted an unnamed source saying that Shakur waved a pistol at Biggie. "Nah, Pac didn't pull steel on me," says Big. "He was on some tough shit, though. I can't knock them dudes for the way they go about their biz. They made everything seem so dramatic. I felt the darkness when he rolled up that night. Duke came out the window fatigued out, screaming 'West Side! Outlaws!' I was, like, 'That's Bishop [Tupac's character in the movie *Juice*]!' Whatever he's doing right now, that's the role he's playing. He played that shit to a tee. He had his little goons with him, and Suge was with him, and they was, like, 'We gonna settle this now.'"

That's when Big's ace, Little Caesar of Junior M.A.F.I.A., stepped up. "The nigga Ceez—pissy drunk—is up on the joint, like, 'Fuck you!'" Big recalls. "Ceez is, like, 'Fuck you, nigga! East Coast muthafucka!' Pac is,

like, 'We on the West Side now, we gonna handle that shit.' Then his niggas start formulating and my niggas start formulating—somebody pulled a gun, muthafuckas start screaming, 'He got a gun, he got a gun!' We're, like 'We're in L.A. What the fuck are we supposed to do, shoot out?' That's when I knew it was on."

But not long after the *Soul Train* incident, it appeared as if Death Row might be starting to chill. At a mid-May East-West "rap summit" in Philadelphia, set up by Dr. Ben Chavis to help defuse the situation, Suge avoided any negative comments about Puffy (who did not attend because he says there was too much hype around the event). "There's nothing between Death Row and Bad Boy, or me and Puffy," said Knight. "Death Row sells volume—so how could Puffy be a threat to me, or Bad Boy be a threat to Death Row?" A few weeks later, however, Death Row released a song that told a different tale.

When Tupac's "Hit 'Em Up"—which mimics the chorus of Junior M.A.F.I.A.'s "Player's Anthem" ("Grab your Glocks when you see Tupac")—hit the streets of New York, damn near every jeep, coupe, and Walkman was pumping it. No fakin' jacks here, son; Tupac set it on the East something lovely. He says he put out the song in retaliation for Big's 1995 "Who Shot Ya," which he took as a comment on his own shooting. "Even if that song ain't about me," he told VIBE, "you should be, like, I'm not putting it out, 'cause he might *think* it's about him.'"

"I wrote that muthafuckin' song way before Tupac got shot," says Big, like he's said it before. "It was supposed to be the intro to that shit Keith Murray was doing on Mary J. Blige's joint. But Puff said it was too hard."

As if the lyrical haymakers thrown at Bad Boy weren't enough, Pac went the extra mile and pulled Mobb Deep into the mix. "Don't one of you niggas got sickle-cell or something?" he says on the record. "You gonna fuck around and have a seizure or a heart attack. You'd better back the fuck up before you smacked the fuck up."

Prodigy of Mobb Deep says he couldn't believe what he heard. "I was like, Oh shit. Them niggas is shittin' on me. He's talking to me about my health. Yo, he doesn't even know me, to be talking about shit like that. I never had any beef with Tupac. I never said his name. So that shit just hurt. I'm like, yeah, all right, whatever. I just gotta handle that shit." Asked what he means by "handling" it, Prodigy replies, "I don't know, son. We gonna see that nigga somewhere and—whatever. I don't know what it's gonna be." In the meantime, the infamous ones plan to include an answer to "Hit 'Em Up" on the B-side of an upcoming single.

In a recent interview with VIBEonline, Tupac summed up his feelings toward Bad Boy in typically dramatic fashion: "Fear got stronger than love, and niggas did things they weren't supposed to do. They know in their hearts—that's why they're in hell now. They can't sleep. That's why they're telling all the reporters and all the people, 'Why they doing this? They fucking up hip hop' and blah-blah-blah, 'cause they in hell. They can't make money, they can't go anywhere. They can't look at themselves, 'cause they know the prodigal son has returned."

In the face of all this, one might wonder why Biggie hasn't retaliated physically to Tupac's threats. After all, he's the same Bed-Stuy soldier who rapped, "C-4 to your door, no beef no more." Says Big, "The whole reason I was being cool from Day One was because of that nigga Puff. 'Cause Puff don't get down like that."

So what about a response on record? "He got the streets riled up because he got a little song dissing me," Big replies, "but how would I look dissing him back? My nigga is, like, 'Fuck dat nigga, that nigga's so much on your dick, it don't even make no sense to say anything."

Given Death Row's intimidating reputation, does Puffy believe that he's in physical danger? "I never knew of my life being in danger," he says calmly. "I'm not saying that I'm ignorant to the rumors. But if you got a problem and somebody wants to get your ass, they don't talk about it. What it's been right now is a lot of moviemaking and a lot of entertainment drama. Bad boys move in silence. If somebody wants to get your ass, you're gonna wake up in heaven. There ain't no record gonna be made about it. It ain't gonna be no interviews; it's gonna be straight-up 'Oh shit, where am I? What are these wings on my back? Your name is Jesus Christ?' When you're involved in some real shit, it's gonna be some real shit.

"But ain't no man gonna make me act a way that I don't want to act. Or make me be something I'm not. I ain't a gangster, so why y'all gonna tell me to start acting like a gangster? I'm trying to be an intelligent black man. I don't give a fuck if niggas think that's corny or not. If anybody comes and touches me, I'm going to defend myself. But I'ma be me—a young nigga who came up making music, trying to put niggas on, handle his business, and make some history."

The history of hip hop is built on battles. But it used to be that when heads had a problem, they could pull a mike and settle it, using hollow-point rhymes to rub their competitors off the map. Well, things done changed. The era of the gun clapper is upon us, with rappers and record execs alike taking their cue from *Scarface*. Meanwhile, those on the sidelines seem less concerned with the truth than with fanning the flames—gossiping about death threats and retribution, lying in wait for the first sign of bloodshed.

When the bloodshed came, it wasn't quite what people expected. On June 30, Puffy was rushed to the emergency room of St. Luke's–Roosevelt Hospital in Upper Manhattan, where he was treated for a deep cut to his lower right arm. New York's *Daily News* called it a "slit wrist," implying that it was more than an accident. Puffy calls the story nonsense. "I was playing with my girl and I reached for a champagne glass and it broke on my bracelet, cutting my arm," he says. "I ain't tryin' to kill myself. I got problems but it ain't that bad."

More than anything, Puffy seems exhausted by the whole ordeal. But after all he's seen in the past two years, nothing can surprise him—except, maybe, the squashing of this beef. "I'm ready for it to be out of my life and be over with. I mean that from the bottom of my heart. I just hope it can end quick and in a positive way, because it's gotten out of hand."

"At first Death Row was just a big family thing," says Dr. Dre. "But the more money that got made, the further apart everybody came. Certain people started becoming what they hated. It was too much negativity. So, from here on out, Death Row Records don't even exist to Dre.

"And about this East Coast—West Coast shit?" he says. "Kill that noise! That's the biggest case of black-on-black crime I've seen in my life."

FREAKY

OCTOBER 1996

As if criminal charges, attempts on his life, bicoastal hip hop conflicts, and a quintuple-platinum album aren't enough, Tupac Shakur is once again making headlines with the music video for his number one rap single "How Do U Want It?" Directed by the adult film world's notorious Ron Hightower, the video is an unprecedented convergence of high-profile porn stars and hip hoppers.

"The video is not just thrown at you," says Hightower, director of such X-rated movies as *Kink World* and *Vivid Raw Three*. "As hard as it may be, I personally feel that it was done with taste."

While it avoids the juvenile rump shaking favored in countless rap clips past, "How Do U Want It?" isn't exactly fit for the casual VH1 viewer. Pairing Tupac and Jodeci's K-Ci and JoJo (who both guest on the song) with erotic film luminaries Heather Hunter, Nina Hartley, and others, the video is stuffed with titillating imagery: Tupac and Hunter sharing a straddle on the saddle of a mechanical bull; go-go-caged naked women engaging in oral favors; and most memorably, a hot-tub sequence in which champagne is poured down the bare torso and crotch of a fetching young woman, right into the wine glass of a thirsty K-Ci.

An alternate, nudity-free version of "How Do U Want It?" was already one of MTV's most requested videos at press time, while the adult version premieres September 14 on the Playboy Channel's *Hot Rocks: Back to School* music video program. Big butt advocate Sir Mix-A-Lot will be hosting the show.

There have been other rappers who've done explicit music videos: Luke, Sir Mix, and most recently, DJ Polo, whose "Freak of the Week" video features John Wayne Bobbitt and porn legend Ron Jeremy. But "How Do U Want It?" manages to be racier and more glamorous than any of these. "Not to sound conceited, but I don't think [anyone else] came with the amount of class that we did," says Hightower. "I definitely see this video creating its own chapter for others to follow." C. DeLores oughta love that.
Chairman Mao

DEAKY

IN THE EVENT OF MY DEMISE

When my heart can beat no more
I hope I die for a principle or a belief that
> *I have lived for*
I will die before my time because I already feel
> *the shadow's depth*
So much I wanted to accomplish before
> *I reached my death*
I have come to grips with the possibility and
> *wiped the last tear from my eyes*
I loved all who were positive in the event
> *of my demise*

> —2Pac, 1992

An unpublished poem he requested be shared with friends after his death

READY TO

And the light shineth in the darkness; and the darkness comprehended it not.

–John 1:5

Day One, Saturday, September 7: Mike Tyson is a thug's champion. Mighty but vulnerable, streetwise but naive, standing in a precarious place despite his wealth. The place is special in the hearts of hustlers. A Tyson fight is an unofficial gangsta party. It's where the ghetto elite meet: rich niggas with nothing to lose, indulging their contradictions.

The anticipation builds as colorfully dressed folks file into the MGM Grand on this hot Las Vegas evening. Inside, playas like Stacey Augmon, New Edition, Gary Payton, Too Short, and Run-D.M.C. settle in. Among the 'bangers, ballers, dealers, and denizens in the VIP section are two of America's most infamous: Marion "Suge" Knight, the Death Row Records CEO who's made no secret of his affiliation with the Bloods, and his quintuple-platinum superstar, Tupac Shakur.

The bell dings, and Mike Tyson makes quick work of a hapless Bruce Seldon. Too quick for the crowd's taste. The mood after the 109-second fight is ugly, but Tupac is gleeful, jumping about like a little boy. "Did you see Tyson do it to 'im? Tyson did it to 'im! Did y'all see that?" says 'Pac, baiting a camera crew in the MGM lobby. He becomes more and

DIE

On September 7, Tupac Shakur was shot four times in a Las Vegas drive-by. Six days later he died. *Rob Marriott* **bears witness to the final days of one of hip hop's brightest and most conflicted stars**

more animated talking about Mike. "Did y'all see that? Fifty punches! I counted, fifty punches! I knew he was gon' take him out. We bad like that. Come out of prison and now we running shit." Suge, smiling at 'Pac's antics, grabs his arm and coaxes him away from the camera.

Tupac returns to his room at the nearby Luxor, a massive black pyramid with a brightly illuminated top. According to a close friend, he's slightly upset because he couldn't find his road dawgs, the Outlaws, who were supposed to be at the fight with him. "He complained of getting into a scrap with some Crips."

Back outside the MGM, an amateur videographer catches 'Pac and Suge waiting for their car, surrounded by a bevy of women.

Tupac has changed from the brushed silk shirt he wore to the fight to a dark green basketball jersey that better exposes his tattooed biceps and the diamond-and-ruby-encrusted medallion hanging from his neck. On it is an angel in waiting, wings outspread, gun in hand.

"Well it's time to ride / I'm ready to die right here tonight / And mother-fuck they life / That's what they screamin' as they drill me / But I'm hard to kill, so open fire."
–2Pac, "Ambitionz az a Ridah"

Eleven-fifteen P.M. finds Suge and 'Pac turning off Las Vegas

117

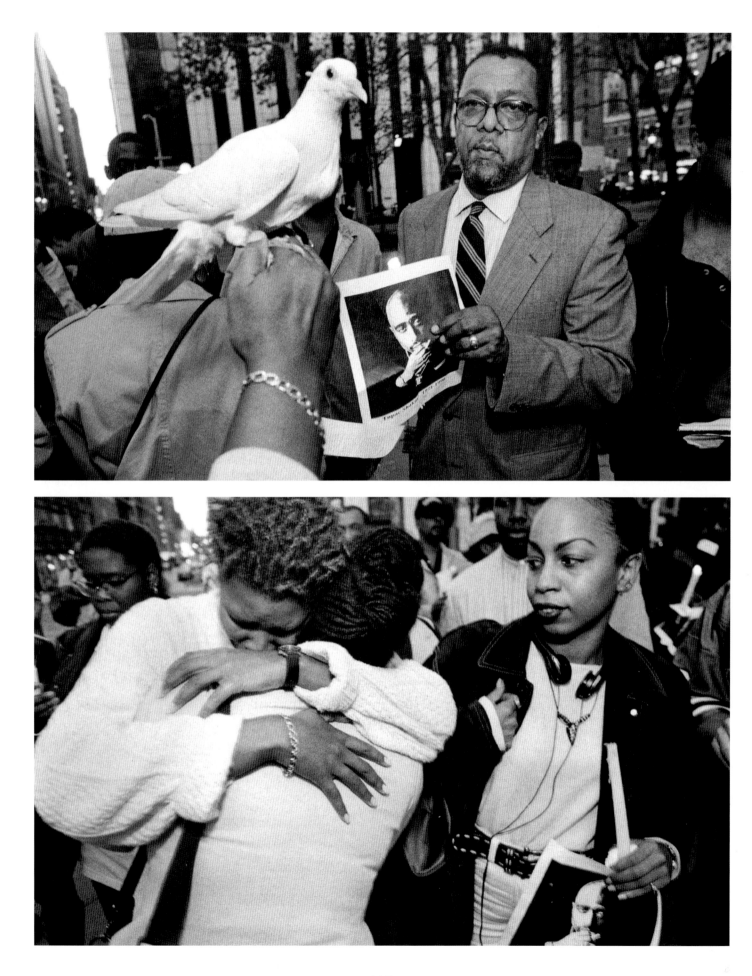

Boulevard onto Flamingo, heading east toward Suge's Club 662 in a black BMW 750, presumably to get their party on. Several women in an Oldsmobile flash 'Pac and Suge. Suge's at the wheel and 'Pac's next to him, his window down. He's all smiles, yelling to his fans, inviting them to join the party. Leading a convoy estimated at anywhere between six and fifteen cars, the BMW stops at a red light in front of the Maxim Hotel—just beyond the Strip, where the neon and hubbub end and the darkness of a desert town begins.

A late-model white Cadillac with California plates pulls up to the right of the BMW. One of its four passengers takes out a high-caliber firearm. "I heard these sounds and thought it was someone shooting in the air," says an eyewitness who was idling three cars back, "but then

in the back of the BMW, bleeding profusely. Sirens wail. Ambulance lights flash. "There was blood everywhere," says one witness.

"Get down!" yells a policeman, pointing a shotgun at Suge.

"I gotta get my boy to the hospital," Suge says.

"Shut up. Get down!" Suge bends his knees to the ground.

Across town, a white Cadillac slips quietly away into the night.

"I'm dying, I'm dying," says Tupac as he's being brought into University Medical Center's intensive care unit. He's lost a lot of blood. He undergoes the first of two complicated operations. Afterwards, Tupac's mother, aunt, and friends—including Mike Tyson, Jasmine Guy, and Jesse Jackson—rush to his side.

Day Two: Within hours the shots have been heard 'round the

I see sparks fly from the gun." Between ten and fifteen shots ring out. Lead pierces metal, glass, flesh. Two bullets tear through Tupac's chest, one through a hand, one in a leg. Bullet fragments graze the top of Suge's head. The Cadillac peels off to the right, heading south down Koval Street. With two tires blown out and the windshield shot through, Suge floors his Beemer, screeching into a wild U-turn against oncoming traffic as vehicles scatter.

Two policemen at the Maxim on an unrelated call hear the shots and see the commotion. They immediately give chase. According to a friend of Suge's, who was told the details later, Tupac is now bleeding through his jersey. "Gotta keep your eyes open," 'Pac says to himself. Suge stops the car and the police arrive. Tupac is stretched out

world. Two years after the last attempt on his life, hip hop's Lazarus has caught bullets once again and no one knows what to think. Will he die? Will he return from this ordeal larger, more invincible? It's difficult to imagine such a kinetic and volatile figure lying immobilized. This, after all, is the same man who got into a gun battle with cops on an Atlanta street and bopped out of the courtroom unscathed. The same man who survived five bullet wounds in a 1994 Times Square ambush. The same man who, though convicted of sexual abuse, left a New York jail richer and more popular than when he went in. " 'Pac will be all right," says a family member. "He'll pull through."

Predictably, the media jumps on the gangsta image, the court cases, the prison terms, and the thuggish lyrics Bob Dole denounced.

But his friends recount other stories. "I've always known him to be gracious, humane," says hip hop mogul Russell Simmons. "All this gangsta stuff, I've never seen it. I remember him dancing with this woman in a wheelchair for four hours when everybody else was drinking and partying. That's how I knew the man. He's a total sophisticate: intelligent, articulate."

"He looks like a sleeping black angel," says a close friend, after visiting Tupac in the hospital. "I talked to him, touched him. I told him to go to his light."

The members of Suge's Death Row entourage are questioned by police, but provide little information. Sergeant Kevin Manning of the Las Vegas Police Department says, "They were not quite candid,"

decide to go in a second time and remove 'Pac's shattered right lung. "You can live with one lung," says Dr. Jonathan Weissler, chief of pulmonary and critical care medicine at Southwestern Medical in Dallas. "And after a while you can live quite well with it."

After hours of unconsciousness, Tupac momentarily opens his eyes. Hearts are lifted.

Day Four: The entire hip hop world is turned on its ear. Overzealous reporters suggest that the shooting is tied to the East Coast–West Coast rivalry. A few speculate that it may be gang-related. Among the names being thrown about are the Notorious B.I.G. and Mobb Deep (who are both entangled in protracted lyric feuds with Tupac), Las Vegas Crips, Los Angeles Crips, even Death Row employees.

about the circumstances surrounding the shooting.

Day Three: Fearing gang-related violence, hospital authorities step up security. Between UMC security, LVPD, and Death Row bodyguards, the trauma unit is all badges, brawn, and walkie-talkies. Outside, a local Channel 3 news van backfires twice and everybody in earshot drops to the ground.

At about 8 P.M., police and Tupac's crew get into a shouting match that results in people getting handcuffed and detained by police. LVPD's Gang Sergeant Cindi West calls it "a misunderstanding."

Rumors abound. Depending on who you ask, Tupac is either on his way to the morgue or in intensive care puffing on a cigarette. In truth, he's alive but experiencing respiratory trouble. Surgeons

At least one Bad Boy Entertainment staffer receives death threats, and the New York–based label cancels a scheduled appearance of some of their artists.

"That this is gang-related is still pure speculation," says Sergeant Manning. "We have to run by facts." The entire Death Row organization, according to one employee, has been put under a gag order by higher-ups. LVPD, frustrated by the lack of cooperation from Tupac's camp, complain to the press. "The problem is a lack of forthrightness," says Manning, barely concealing his disgust. "It amazes me when they have professional bodyguards who can't even give an accurate description of the vehicle." Meanwhile Suge, who was released from the hospital with minor head wounds, is nowhere to be found.

In the trauma unit there's meditation and prayer. Tupac's aunt, Yaasmyn Fula, a tall, regal woman, removes her glasses and wipes her puffy eyes. "I'm just really, really tired," she says quietly. Afeni Shakur, 50, a woman of small frame and formidable grace, looks about the same. The former Black Panther whom 'Pac calls Mama seems to carry the weight of the world upon her small shoulders. Visiting hours are almost over and she returns to the hotel for an hour or two of restless rest. 'Pac is still in critical condition.

Family members silently get into a plain blue Chrysler. An older man holds Afeni, and she leans in heavily as the car drives away.

Day Five: The morning brings news of a murder in Los Angeles. A Compton bodyguard, who police say is connected with the Southside Crips, has been shot in his car and pronounced dead at Martin Luther King Jr. General Hospital at 9:53 A.M. The rumor is that the homicide was payback for Tupac being shot. "Someone just drove up alongside and blasted him," says LAPD homicide detective Mike Pariz. "This is only the beginning," says a Compton resident. "The gang shit is about to be on."

Suge makes himself available to the LVPD for questioning. Investigators review a videotape from the MGM taken the night of the Tyson fight, which reportedly shows Tupac and others in a confrontation with an unknown black man. "This happened at approximately 8:45 P.M.," says Sergeant Manning. "Kicking and punching were involved." Authorities won't reveal whether Tupac or Suge personally assaulted the man. Once police officers arrived at the scene they asked if the victim wanted to file a complaint. He said "Forget it" and walked away. Officers never got a name. "There is no reason to believe that these incidents are at all connected," says Manning.

Day Six: Tupac, his eyes closed and his remaining lung inflamed, struggles for his life. He's connected to a respirator, his body convulsing violently at times. Doctors induce paralysis for fear of 'Pac hurting himself. Dr. John Fildes, chairman of the hospital's trauma center, gives him a 20 percent chance of survival. "It's a very fatal injury," he says. "A patient may die from lack of oxygen or may bleed to death."

Despite newspaper headlines like WOUNDED TUPAC IS UNLIKELY TO LIVE, family members hold out hope.

Day Seven: "This is Dale Pugh, marketing and public relations director for the University Medical Center," says a hospital hotline answering machine. "This message is being recorded at approximately 5:15 P.M. on Friday, September 13. Tupac Shakur has passed away at UMC at approximately 4:03 p.m. Physicians have listed the cause of death as respiratory failure and cardiopulmonary arrest."

At the hospital there's a stillness, a surreal calm. The contradictions of Tupac's many worlds are converging. More than 150 people are gathered out front: dark young girls and their mothers, lanky young men with combs in their uncombed heads; others wearing do-rags, professional women, young Native American 'bangers and children—dozens and dozens of children. Detached reporters wait with the teary-eyed.

Surrounded by family, Afeni dashes out of the trauma unit, quiet determination etched on her face. "She is an extremely spiritual person," says a family friend. "I think she knew. She had given her only son to God long before this day."

A member of Tupac's crew leaves the trauma room soon after. He stares down a hospital staffer and screams: "Why the fuck you let him die, yo? Why the fuck you let him die?"

Behind him, Yakki, Tupac's cousin, who's been at 'Pac's side since forever, walks out, red in the face. Death Row artist Danny Boy comes in tube socks and slippers, tears falling from behind half-and-half glasses. He bends down on one knee as if in prayer.

There's a trace of crimson in the clouds. Suddenly three shining cars appear and Suge Knight steps out of a black Lexus in a Phoenix Suns T-shirt, the wound up top his head barely noticeable. His massive figure quiets the crowd. He enters the trauma center hugging

Danny Boy around the neck and talking quietly with members of Tupac's family. Without his running mate Tupac, Suge seems more solitary. After a few minutes he turns to leave, taking pulls on a barely lit cigar and leaving whispers in his wake.

As the minutes go by, an almost festive atmosphere develops outside. Cars roll up bumping Tupac songs. Children begin running beyond their mothers' reach. One little boy in naps and slippers plays dead in the street.

The press packs it up. The crowd begins to disperse. A black Humvee circles the hospital, blaring "If I Die Tonight":

"I'll live eternal / Who shall I fear / Don't shed a tear for me nigga /

I ain't happy here." The resoluteness in 'Pac's voice is cathartic. "I hope they bury me and send me to my rest / Headlines readin' murdered to death / My last breath . . ."

Such eerily prophetic lines were not unusual for Tupac, who seemed to be rehearsing his death from early on. For him, it was valor over violence, destiny over death. But if his listeners were forewarned, they were still unprepared. "Now it's real," says one hip hop journalist. "This scene has lost its cherry. All the shit people have been talking in the past five years, all the dissing and posturing, has led to this. Hip hop has crossed a line, and it's gonna be hard to cross back."

LAST TESTAMENT

Two weeks before his death in Las Vegas, Tupac Shakur was in Los Angeles finishing the movie *Gang Related,* in which he plays a corrupt cop. During a break in the filming, he sat down in his trailer with *Rob Marriott* for what may have been his last—and most outrageous—in-depth interview.

the charts. My album cost more than any album you could buy on the charts, and I outsold every one of them muthafuckas. And I did it in two months!

I'm not dissin' niggas blindly. I'm dissin' niggas that opened up they mouth. I aspire not to be a reactionary muthafucka. I read. That's all I do is read. I read books, I read magazines, I read y'all's shit. I listen to everything a muthafucka says, no matter how slight, no matter how long ago he said it. Like, when I was in jail, niggas had a lot to say. When I came home, niggas had a lot to say. I remembered all of it.

Are you motivated by revenge?

Now, it's for fun. This new Makaveli album I got comin' out, I'm takin' on niggas. It's like, my dopest album ever. It's twelve tracks. I talk about my shooting [in New York]. I say the names of the niggas that shot me, the names of the niggas that set me up. . . . Everything I couldn't say, I said it in a rap. I also dis Dre, I dis Mobb Deep. All them niggas: Jaÿ–Z, Puffy, Biggie. My album cover is me on the cross being crucified, and the cross is the map. It's got New York, Harlem, Brooklyn, everything. And I'm on the cross bein' crucified for keepin' it real.

So is it true you got Dre pushed off Death Row?

I did. Suge is the boss of Death Row, the don, you understand? But I'm the underboss, the capo. That's my job, to do what's best for all of Death Row. My decision wasn't based on comin' to Death Row and taking shit over. My decision was based on Dre not being there for Snoop during his trial.

But also, other niggas was producing beats, and Dre was gettin' the credit. And I got tired of that. He was owning the company too and he chillin' in his house; I'm out here in the streets, whoopin' niggas' asses, startin' wars and shit, droppin' albums, doin' my shit, and this nigga takin' three years to do one song! I couldn't have that. But it was not my decision. Suge was comin' to me.

Death Row can never be weak, no matter what. If we stop sellin' millions and all that, we will always have our honor. We will always have our respect, and that's all I'm back in this rap game for. I already have famous records; I'm in this shit for the honor and respect. To be a family, to be known as something, to get this dark cloud off us as a race. We need some kind of sunshine, some kind of exceptional being so we can stop suckin' Malcolm X and Michael Jordan's dick.

Do you and Suge both feel the same way about taking over, not turning back, and not being pawns?

Nobody respects a man who don't do for himself. I'm a soldier; so I'm here on Death Row to put my time into this army. It's not like they got me out of jail and now I gotta do for them. It's that they believed in me, so I believe in this company when no one else will. When people said this was played out. I'm breathin' into it. I don't give a fuck if I don't get along with anybody else on the label. This is for Death Row. When it comes to the point when I feel it can stand on its own, I will move on. But me and Suge will always do business together, forever.

Y'all are kindred spirits?

Everything I don't have, he's got, and everything he don't got, I got. Together, I think we can only be stopped by each other. We want, not oppression, but total domination.

I'm not no dumb-ass muthafucka. I don't bang for the color or the land. It's for the principles, for the honor. I'm banging for the

A re you where you wanna be right now in your career?

I'm at a point where I'm in charge. I don't have to answer to anybody; I'm in total control. I've got another album droppin' next month under an alias name, under Makaveli. It's called *Killuminati*. I'm not the king, I'm not the teacher or nothin' like that, but I feel like I don't have no peers. I've been out less than a year, convicted of allegations that usually end niggas' careers. Shot five times in the nuts and the head. I came out, and in less than a fuckin' year outsold Biggie almost three times. I sold more records than his whole fuckin' record label.

What's with this Makaveli? Why name yourself after a sixteenth-century politician and philosopher?

That's what got me here, my reading. It's not like I idolize this one guy Machiavelli. I idolize that type of thinking where you do whatever's gonna make you achieve your goal.

So now I'm not on no bullshit or anything, I'm gonna change the rules in this rap game. You know how, like, in politics, the Republicans are in now; well, I represent that style; I'm the new nigga. I'ma shake up the whole Congress. By puttin' out a double album–that nobody ever did–I had the most expensive album on

Wesside. It's in my heart. When I be throwing up the *W*, it ain't for California, it's a *W* for war. When the West Coast and the middle and the East get together, we got power. You won't be seeing me throwing this when we're all together. But we ain't there, we still all separate tribes, and I know what tribe I'm in. I'm a soldier. I'll always be true to those who are true to me. New York shouldn't be trippin', they should be loving this, because they gave me the game to do this. What made me raw is that I got both. I'm the future of black America.

Why do you think people always supported you, even in the ugliest situations?

I don't know. All I can say is I always try to be a real nigga in my heart. Sometimes it's good, sometimes it's bad; but it's still us. It's never to hurt nobody. I'm not gonna take advantage of you or bully you. I'm on some underdog shit. And I truly believe I've been blessed by God, and God walks with me. Me and my niggas are on some Black Jesus shit. Not a new religion or anything, but the saint for thugs and gangstas—not-killers and rapists, but thugs. When I say thugs, I mean niggas who don't have anything.

I lived and almost died for Thug Life. And after that VIBE article, people said "Tupac, I thought Thug Life was dead." Yeah, but read the rest of the article. Puffy, in that letter in VIBE, gave me some advice that brought me back to the Thug Life shit. He said you can't be a thug for a second or a minute and get in and out of it,

times platinum, but nobody's gon' let them sign no bills. They can't make no hip hop laws.

So what is the source of this power?

I tried to see if it was, like, a white thing. Everywhere I go with money, they let me in. Everywhere I go with none, they don't let you in. Trust me. That's all it is. It's all about money. When you got money, you got power. I guarantee if people keep supportin' me—just buyin' my record, just goin' to my concerts—I'ma keep givin' money. Every time I go platinum I'm puttin' money up for community centers. Every time I go platinum, somebody's gettin' a big check. I feel like an elected official.

You know what I thought when I was in jail, I was, like, No politician is even gettin' at us. I represent five million fuckin' sales. And no politician is even checkin' for us. But by the next election I promise I'll be sitting across from all the candidates. I promise you! I'ma be so far from where I am now in four years—God willin' I'm alive—it's on! I guarantee we will have our own political party. It won't just be for blacks. It's gon' be for Mexicans, for Armenians, all you lost-tribe muthafuckas. We need to have our own political party 'cause we all have the same muthafuckin' problems. We built this nation and we get none of the benefits.

What distinguishes you from everybody else?

I never thought I was the best rapper—the best nothin'. I think I'm the realest nigga out there. I do think that. I think I own that. 'Cause I

BY THE NEXT ELECTION, I'LL BE SITTING ACROSS FROM ALL THE CANDIDATES. I'MA BE SO FAR FROM WHERE I AM NOW IN FOUR YEARS—GOD WILLIN' I'M ALIVE—IT'S ON!

you gotta be in it forever. He didn't mean it as advice at the time, he said it to dampen things. So now, when I'm whoopin' his mutha-fuckin ass, and it hurts, and all these people talkin' about "Stop, now," remember what he told me. These words came out of his mouth.

Biggie's playing it like you got it confused, that he didn't have nothin' to do with your getting shot. . . .

I have no mercy in war. I said in the beginning I was gonna take these niggas out the game, and sure enough I will. Already people can't look at Biggie and not laugh. I took every piece of his power. Anybody who tries to help them, I will destroy. Anyone who wanna side with them or do a record with them, whatever, try to unify with them, I'ma destroy. I swear to God. Can't nobody touch me right now. Maybe next month all of this will be over, but this month I'm takin' every moving target out.

Black people put all their political energies, everything they have, into get-ting loot. Like, right now, it's the presidential campaign. . . .

And we ain't doin' shit.

We're voting on Tupac and Biggie, 'cause that's where we live. Who's gonna get dead presidents, not who's going to be president.

But see, rap is like a politician's race. If I lost New York, I won the other forty-nine states, and that makes me in control. Now I'm the new president for the next four years. Crucial Conflict could go five

think being real is just being true. I'm the nigga that will wear a suit when everybody's got on khakis. I'll be baldheaded when every-body's wearing braids. I'll wear braids when they all baldheaded. It's just being real. I don't have insecurities—well, I do, but I just put them in front of everybody, like my mom and my life and me being little.

We got to kill this niggeritis. Niggas hate me just 'cause of what you doin', niggas plotting on you 'cause of women, and niggas hatin' to see you shine. We got to kill that. Before we can kill it in our black nation, we got to kill it in the Hip Hop Nation, and that's what I'm doin'. It's the only reason I'm back: to bring the heat. And I feel like God is tellin' me to do it. I feel like Black Jesus is controlling me. He's our saint that we pray to; that we look up to. Drug dealers, they sin-ning, right? But they'll be millionaires. How I got shot five times—only a saint, only Black Jesus, only a nigga that know where I'm com-ing from, could be, like, "You know what? He's gonna end up doing some good." I gotta do that.

People might be, like, "This nigga's conceited," but fuck it. I feel like I shine. And I don't give a fuck how much white people, the media, niggas, black people, playa haters, police, whoever, try to darken my shine, I'ma always shine through. They could lie about my words, but they always gonna ring true 'cause it's my essence; it's in my essence, and that's what's always gonna come through.

HOME AT LAST

Tupac Shakur finally died on September 13, 1996, but death had been twitching in his ear for a long time. Shakur was rushed through boyhood only to enter a longish, violent adolescence that ended with bullets dancing through his body, disintegrating organs, dismissing life.

Shakur was a self-proclaimed thug. A macho tantrum thrower embarrassed by the limp of his thoughtfulness. He loved to act but was ashamed of his talent. Back when I knew him, conversations with Tupac often ended with the other person convincing him of his own humanity.

I remember Tupac best as an elated young man with his first real apartment, a one-bedroom joint in Oakland. It was 1991, and Tupac had just returned from a worldwide (hotel after hotel) tour. Before that, he'd often slept on recording studio couches and on the floors of various apartments rented by members of Digital Underground. But he had some tour money left over, and some dough from appearing on the record and in the video for DU's "Same Song."

'Pac's new place had wall-to-wall carpet, and milling about the tiny kitchen was a pretty, cedar-colored young woman, as well as new flatware and dishes. Tupac showed us all around, pointing out this knickknack and that, telling us for how much and from where he purchased his sheets and towels, telling us without telling us of his profound relief at having a place of his own. He'd asked us to stop by, a group of six or eight people, because, at some point, we'd all fed him. He was the baby of the crew; we'd all picked him up from desolate bus stops in the middle of the night, listened to his poems before they were raps, and introduced him to girls we thought were somehow better than the ones he knew.

So we ooohed and aaahed and bounced our butts on the new couch, and bugged when we noticed the two big guns on the lower tier of the glass-top coffee table. The firearms sat there like dried piles of shit—not stinking, but still foul. The guys checked coolly around them with sideways looks and set their feet apart for better balance. The girls stared, left the room, or quietly moved outside onto the tiny cement porch.

Tupac was the baby, the sweetest; but some of us had seen him altercate with state troopers in Oklahoma, confront (over bullshit) killer dope dealers in Marin City, and terrify drive-thru workers at fast-food spots all over the country. Tupac was beautiful to look at, a pleasure to chill with. But we all kind of knew he was ready to die. If you were trying to adjust to the world and the ways it mistreated you, 'Pac was a hard brother to be around. He was not trying to adjust. He was calling you out, grabbing you by the sleeve, taking you with him—on missions both stupid and shrewd. *At least pretend to be real,* he seemed to say. *Sucka punk bitch, fuck these mothafuckas! I don't give a fuck* is what he said.

Rowdy with pride, Tupac picked up one of the guns and turned it around in his hands, inspecting its barrel and trigger, bragging excitedly about its ability to do damage. The cedar-colored girl came out of the kitchen with drinks on a tray. It was fruit punch served in new, unwashed glasses, and we endured Tupac's big talk and big guns while flecks of dust and cardboard floated atop our drinks.

No one said anything. It was a combination of tact and trepidation that made us pretend to sip the gritty liquid and watch as Tupac, gun in hand, began to bounce off the walls of his new kingdom. He'd broken a slight sweat, and took a sip of the juice himself. Tupac was thrilled with new money, new things, a new girl, and two guns. On that day, Tupac Shakur was happy to be alive. *Danyel Smith*

ALL THAT GLITTERS

Tupac Shakur is dead and his killer is still on the loose. Suge Knight is in jail and his associates are under fire. As the $300 million Death Row empire crumbles, the ugly truth about the biggest rap label in history is just beginning to emerge. A tragic and twisted turn-of-the-millennium morality tale. *By Rob Marriott*

MAY 1997

Additional reporting by
Choice One, David Bry, Victor Cook, and Linda Hackett

Tupac Amaru Shakur, hip hop's shining serpent, was gone. And now, so was Bobby Ray Finch. Under a cloudless stretch of L.A. sky, Finch's friends and family made the mournful circuit around Inglewood Cemetery. Low-flying planes swept tremendous shadows over the somber procession of mothers and off-duty officers, neighbors and fellow bodyguards, former gang members and present-day *cholos*, a girlfriend robbed of a lover, a daughter robbed of a father, and a reporter trying his best to look inconspicuous at an intimate family gathering.

I'd been covering the story since September 7, 1996, when a hail of bullets tore into Tupac's body for the second and final time in his brief life. Now, on September 18, six days after

Shakur's death, I looked on as, one by one, Bobby Finch's family filed by and stared into his lifeless face. The carnations lying on the casket, as well as the casket itself, were baby blue, seeming to confirm reports that Bobby was a member of a "marked" gang, the Southside Crips, and was killed in retaliation for Tupac's shooting.

On the morning of September 11, Finch, age 30, was murdered in front of his mama's house in Compton while sitting at the wheel of his new Acura. He had just dropped off his 10-year-old daughter at school and was heading to the gym for a workout. According to a witness, a Honda Civic hatchback pulled up alongside Finch, and shots were fired. He was taken to Martin Luther King Jr. Medical Center with multiple chest wounds and pronounced dead minutes after arrival.

"This was a case of mistaken identity. Bobby wasn't no gangbanger. He wasn't part of that lifestyle," said Leshaun Smith, godfather of Bobby's daughter, in frustration. "Look," he told me, "if you live in an area, you know people. Around here, if somebody in a neighborhood does somethin' wrong, the entire neighborhood will suffer the consequences. The whole neighborhood is at risk.

"When the gangs do shit like this, they go after the ballers," explained Leshaun [**baller** \ bol'ah\ *n* **1:** high-rolling hustler **2:** nigga that got his money right, as opposed to a banger, who works in blood and bullets]. "They aim to take out the money first. Because Bobby had a nice car, they assumed he was a baller. He was a bodyguard, but he didn't work for none of them rappers. He had nothing to do with any of this."

Whether Finch was a banger, a baller, or neither, didn't matter as much as the fact that certain people perceived him to be connected to a set. In the frenzied days after Tupac's shooting on the Las Vegas Strip, word spread that one of Compton's Southside Crips had fired the shots at Shakur and Death Row Records CEO Marion "Suge" Knight, who grew up in Lueders Park, Compton, among Mob Piru Bloods. Soon after, rumors began to circulate that an eerie, hyphenated order had been issued: "Crip-a-Day."

Whatever the case, a burgeoning gang war was erupting on the streets of Compton in mid-September. Various Crip and Blood sets aligned themselves in preparation for battle: Southside joined forces with Kelly Park, Atlantic Drive, and Neighborhood Crips; Mob Pirus joined up with Lueders Park and Elm Lane Pirus.

Finch was one of three fatalities among 13 shootings police say resulted from the attack on Shakur and Knight. The two other dead men, Timothy Flanagan and Marcus Childs, were believed to be Piru Bloods. One of the survivors, a Southside Crip leader named Darnell Brim, was ambushed in a convenience store and shot several times. An innocent bystander, 10-year-old Lakezia McNeese, caught a stray bullet in the back. When the shooter approached Brim's fallen body, gun outstretched to finish the job, he saw Lakezia's wounded form lying beneath Brim's. He paused and then walked away without firing.

As I stood in the back of the church at Finch's funeral, listening to a young woman sing the last stanzas of "Precious Lord," someone grabbed me by the arm and pulled me out of the service. He was a hulking, off-duty LAPD officer, one of several cops regularly employed by Death Row as security guards. He recognized me as one of the reporters who'd stood vigil outside the Vegas hospital where Tupac took his final breaths.

"What are you doing here?" he whispered, his eyes darting.

Just trying to find out what's going on.

"I hope you realize you're playing a dangerous game."

What you mean?

"Just be careful with what you write."

And so it has gone for the past few months. Cryptic warnings. Demanded anonymity. Lies and whispers. Few in L.A. have been willing to speak on record about anything relating to the ongoing Death Row saga. Vegas police have alternately affirmed and denied that they have any suspects in Tupac's murder. They have yet to arrest anyone, even though a 29-year-old Compton resident named Orlando Anderson was reportedly heard bragging about his involvement days after the shooting.

There are no easy answers to the myriad questions surrounding Tupac's death. But it has become clear that the rap star's killing—and the three homicides that followed—are only the most visible tragedies in a tangled web of intrigue that extends deep into the L.A. underworld—a place where entertainers, cops, gangstas, lawyers, and bodyguards coexist in the same shadowy milieu of nepotism and corruption. It's still very much the wild, wild west out here, and the truth, especially the bloody truth, is hard to come by.

Since February 28, when Suge Knight caught a nine-year bid, everything you thought you knew about Death Row has been thrown into question. Did Knight really build the $300 million empire from the ground up, or was start-up money provided by an incarcerated drug kingpin? Was Knight really the man calling the shots, or was it his attorney, David Kenner? And was Knight so short on cash that mortgaging Death Row's assets to its distributor, Interscope Records, was his only option?

You blew it," said L.A. Superior Court Judge J. Stephen Czuleger when he sentenced Knight to nine years in prison for his role in an attack on Orlando Anderson the night of Tupac's shooting. "You really had everything going for you. The problem is, you have engaged over the years in one thing that causes me grave concern . . . and that is the danger element."

At age 31, Knight has been convicted on eight occasions for a variety of weapons and assault charges. The one-time baller extraordinaire is likely to serve about four years of the nine-year sentence. Meanwhile, the FBI and other federal agencies are investigating Death Row for money laundering and involvement with drugs. They also have questions about Suge's investments in the now defunct Vegas nightclub Club 662, which, allegedly, has had extensive ties to organized crime. On February 13, a federal grand jury subpoenaed the financial records of Knight, Kenner, Death Row, and 36 other individuals and companies who have done business with them. (Neither Knight nor Kenner agreed to be interviewed for this piece.)

The youngest of three children and the only boy, Marion "Sugar Bear" Knight Jr. was raised in a solidly working-class neighborhood by Maxine and Marion Knight Sr., a truck driver and part-time R&B singer from Mississippi. Suge went from a star defensive tackle at the University of Nevada, Las Vegas, to bodyguard and gofer for the likes of Bobby Brown and Dr. Dre, to vainglorious head-nigga-in-charge of the most successful rap label in history. Now the man with the infamous red double-breasted is one of about six thousand incarcerated in L.A. County Men's Central Jail, dressed to the neck in county blues.

Even behind bars, Suge's largesse is legendary. While serving his first month in County, he bought out the commissary every day, allowing the other inmates to eat, drink, and smoke for free. His generosity is a sorely underexposed side of this self-made mogul. In their mad dash for the sensational, the media missed the Hawaii trips for poor kids in Compton, the holiday turkey giveaways, the Mother's Day extravaganzas. Still, the generosity, like all Suge's moves, is rooted in what street folk call game [**game** \gam\ *n* 1: that complex of hustler dos and don'ts, jailhouse rites, and street understanding 2: the very closest thing to Wesside ghetto cosmology—as described on E-40's latest LP, *Tha Hall of Game*].

"Suge doesn't run by business rules," says a former employee of Death Row Records. "His law is the law of the streets. Remember when he said on *Prime Time Live* that he would never tell the police if he knew who [killed Tupac]? That's the game." For Suge, game was something of a religion, the undercurrent of his every action. Sometimes these actions have seemed benign—organizing Death Row as a Mafia-style family, giving back heftily to the community—sometimes they've been suspect. The now deceased Ruthless Records president, Eazy-E, retired rapper Vanilla Ice, and various others have charged that Suge used threats and physical intimidation to force them into signing away potential millions.

In the ganglands of L.A., the line between victor and victim is thin. Success makes you a target. What few understood about Suge was that his tougher-than-tough image was not just bravado but a kind of self-protective instinct run amok. For Suge, being ruthless went with the territory, be it corporate America or the violent streets of Compton. "I seen people slapped up, punked, forced out into the cold in their underwear," says another former Death Row employee. The stories multiplied, the legend grew: brutal beatdowns in his blood-red Tarzana studio and offices, attack dogs and piranha tanks, pistol whippings, veiled and unveiled threats to any and everyone that crossed him.

So, by late 1995, when Suge and his consigliere David Kenner went to visit Shakur in a New York jail, offering bail money and a handwritten contract, Tupac was well aware of Knight's infamy. Not that 'Pac was one to shy away from trouble. Two years before the fatal Vegas gunshots, the heavily tattooed flesh of his torso already told a horror tale in braille, and his volatile words and actions clearly reflected his anger. Adding 'Pac to Death Row's roster was like adding brimstone to fire.

So verily, verily the man in the blood-red suit came and offered him the world. Diamonds, limos, and hoochies versus trying to keep hope alive in a jail cell. 'Pac didn't think twice. For many who supported him through his travails, Tupac's move to Death Row was the beginning of the end. "We felt he sold his soul," said one family friend. "But he would say, from behind the glass, 'I have to get out of here,' and what could you say to that?"

Upon Tupac's release from jail and the debut of his seven-times platinum double album *All Eyez on Me*, Suge and 'Pac formed what proved to be an unholy alliance. Ever looking for the next nigga to bitch, Suge was busy tormenting his East Coast nemesis, Puffy Combs, while 'Pac was provoking the Notorious B.I.G. and helping push Dre off the label he supposedly co-owned. It was 'Pac's way, he said, of "putting in work" for the Row [**putting in work** \'put'ing 'in 'werk\ *v* 1: doing whatever's necessary to add to the riches and notoriety of your set 2: to put the set's needs before your own].

Tupac seemed finally to have found a cause for all his misplaced valor. Between the money, male ritualizing, and the perpetual spotlight, Death Row gave him the chance to actualize his fantasies. "If he wrote it, he lived up to it," says Kendrick Wells, a friend from Tupac's Marin City days. "Some guys do stuff, then write about it. 'Pac would write about it, then be it."

As the months passed and the magazine covers multiplied, Suge and 'Pac fed each other's illusions, and the architecture of their public personas became downright gothic. 'Pac became hip hop's enfant terrible, the Capo Makaveli, and Suge, the black Mafia Don—equal parts Al Capone and Tommy Mottola. In late 1996, with a stroke of inspired hubris, Suge renamed the company the New "Untouchable" Death Row, tempting gangsta and God alike. And then one neon-lit September night, Suge found himself making a wild U-turn on the Las Vegas Strip, his Beemer shot the fuck up, his biggest star bullet-riddled and bleeding in the backseat.

The spray of lead that took Tupac's life had been a long time coming—but it wasn't coming from where most of the media suspected. Numerous reporters, quick to vilify hip hop music, assumed that the shooting was related to the highly publicized feud between East (Bad Boy) and West (Death Row). But any evidence implicating Puffy and Biggie was slim at best: According to police, they had been known to enlist members of the Southside Crips—who'd been feuding with the Mob Piru Bloods for years—as personal security.

But among Compton residents and police informants, one name kept coming up in connection with Shakur's fatal shooting: Orlando Napolian Anderson, also known as Baby Lando, a reputed Southside Crip from nearby Lakewood.

According to a Compton police affidavit, the stage was set for 'Pac's murder approximately two months earlier when some Crips and Bloods ran into one another at the Lakewood Mall. Travon Lane (a.k.a. Tray), a five-foot-four Mob Piru who was wearing a diamond-encrusted Death Row pendant, was in the mall's Foot Locker store with fellow Pirus Kevin Woods (a.k.a. K.W.) and Maurice Combs (a.k.a. Lil' Mo) when they were confronted by seven to eight Southside Crips. The two crews got into it, and Tray's pendant was taxed.

On September 7, Tray attended the Mike Tyson–Bruce Seldon fight with Suge, Tupac, and other members of Death Row. After the fight, Tray recognized Orlando Anderson in the MGM Grand Hotel lobby as one of the Crips who stole his pendant. 'Pac, ever the soldier, stepped up to Lando and asked, "You from the South?" It became a rhetorical question when 'Pac and the crew got to kicking and stomping Anderson into the ground. Shakur, it seems, had finally crossed the line from gangsta rapper to official L.A. gang member. According to the police affidavit, he had recently added a MOB tattoo to one of his heavily illustrated arms.

The melee, broken up by MGM security, was recorded by the hotel's surveillance cameras. Security personnel advised the victim, identified only as "Orlando," to file a report. He refused and soon left the hotel. About three hours later, Suge and 'Pac were in Knight's black BMW 750, leading a caravan of cars along the Strip. While they idled at a red light, a late-model white Cadillac rode up alongside.

"We was at the light," Suge told police some days later. "We was havin' a conversation; heard some gunshots. We looked to the right of us. Tupac was tryin' to get in the backseat. . . . I grabbed him and pulled him down. It was about fifteen gunshots." Police reports said that shell casings from a Glock .40-caliber were recovered from the scene.

Investigators turned up leads 220 miles to the southwest, in L.A., where gang members had already begun exchanging gunfire. An informant told cops that on September 9, two days after 'Pac's shooting, he'd seen a Southside Crip by the name of Jerry "Monk" Bonds driving a late-model white Cadillac into an automotive shop at White and Alondra in Compton. On September 10, cops saw Monk and Orlando Anderson drive to 1315 Glencoe Avenue, a known Southside Crip safe house and hangout. Police raided the Glencoe duplex that same day, recovering seven ski masks, an assault rifle, and a large amount of ammunition, including Smith & Wesson .40-caliber rounds. They also found photos of gang members and a black duffel bag with a Southwest Airlines baggage tag bearing a Las Vegas address.

Anderson wasn't at the duplex when the cops broke in, but Monk was. When interviewed by police, Monk correctly identified every Southside Crip in a recovered photo except Anderson, for whom he gave a false name. When the cops later asked him why he had lied about Anderson's identity, Monk said, "Because he's my cousin."

At 9:15 a.m. the next day, September 11, Bobby Finch was killed, and Compton police were on high alert. That evening, they responded to a tip that several Southside Crips were loading guns into a house at a nearby Compton location. When the cops arrived, they found Anderson and four other suspected Crips standing in the front yard. Anderson ran into the house pursued by police. Several weapons were confiscated from the house, including an AK-47 assault rifle, a .38-caliber revolver, two shotguns, a .9mm M-11 assault pistol, and assorted ammunition. Police also found a diploma with Anderson's name on it hanging in the bedroom. But Anderson denied knowing who lived in the house, insisting that he resided next door with his uncle, Dwayne Keith Davis (a.k.a. Keefee D), a Southside Crip.

In the following weeks, as the shootings multiplied, the L.A. gang unit, along with the FBI and BATF, organized a massive sweep of Blood and Crip neighborhoods. In the predawn hours of October 2, some 300 agents clad in black masks, helmets, and bullet-proof vests burst into 37 homes and arrested 23 people, including Anderson. He was taken into custody on an outstanding warrant, which stemmed from an April '96 murder in Compton—unrelated to Tupac's death. Anderson was released two days later for lack of evidence.

Anderson's attorney, Edi Faal, has acknowledged that his client was assaulted by the Death Row crew at the MGM Grand, but denies that Anderson had anything to do with Shakur's death. Las Vegas police, who initially said that Anderson was one of a handful of people under investigation for Tupac's murder, now say he's no longer a suspect. "We have no one who has talked to us that can tell us more than 'Orlando did it,'" said Detective Brent Becker of the Las Vegas police department. "If I say John Doe killed President Kennedy, does that mean he did it? If someone tells me that you killed Kennedy, is it fair to call you a suspect?"

Whether or not Shakur's family and friends believe Anderson was involved, they've criticized both the department and its investigation. In late February, two of Tupac's associates—his former bodyguard Frank Alexander and fellow rapper Malcolm Greenridge (a.k.a. E.D.I Mean)—told the *L.A. Times* they saw the men who shot Tupac but have never been asked to identify any suspects. "Could I identify the killer of my friend Tupac Shakur if the police showed me photos or a lineup of suspects? Possibly so," said Alexander, who was traveling in the car directly behind Tupac when he was shot.

Sgt. Kevin Manning of the Las Vegas police department said that the statements Alexander and Greenridge gave the police the night of the shooting were inconsistent with what they later told the *L.A. Times*. "We would welcome their additional information and are surprised that they haven't contacted us sooner," said Manning.

However, those closest to Tupac claim the cops aren't really interested in finding his shooter. "It was clear to me from Day One," says 'Pac's mother, Afeni Shakur, "that the Las Vegas police never had any intention of solving the case of my son's murder."

Vegas police maintain that their investigation has been hampered by uncooperative witnesses and a general lack of solid evidence. "We've had aliens from outer space; we've had the ghosts of mob people named as suspects," says Becker. "We've even had people call and say Tupac's still alive. Trust me, he's dead—I was present at the autopsy."

The People vs. Marion Knight. On the morning of October 22, Suge sat in Room 109 of the L.A. Superior Courthouse, Judge John W. Ouderkirk presiding. It was the first of several hearings to determine whether Suge had violated his probation by allegedly smoking marijuana and traveling to the Bahamas without notifying state authorities. He'd been on probation since 1995 after pleading no contest to charges that he pistol-whipped and threatened the lives of aspiring rappers Lynwood and George Stanley in 1992.

Ouderkirk looked annoyed as David Kenner tried to explain away his client's various probation violations as miscommunications and bureaucratic snafus. The judge seemed openly disgusted when he finally addressed Knight in tones befitting a gangsta. "Mr. Knight has run out his string of excuses," he said. "Probation is a privilege to be honored. What we have here before the court is a failure to honor that privilege. I find it ironic that Mr. Knight told his victim on the evening of the attack, 'When I say do something, you do it.' It seems Mr. Knight likes to make those orders but cannot follow them."

Before Suge was escorted to his cell, Sharitha Knight, his wife and head of his management company, rose from her seat. "David," she asked, "can he see his daughter?" No one answered. The little girl, with Juicy Fruit in one pocket, a pack of M&Ms in the other, stood quietly by her bodyguard, her tiny hand swallowed whole by his. She seemed unfazed as her daddy was led from the room.

In a subsequent probation hearing on November 26, the surveillance video of Orlando Anderson's beatdown at the MGM Grand became critical evidence. Suge had been recorded among the pack, though it was difficult to see whether he was delivering blows or, as he claimed, trying to intervene.

Orlando Anderson, the man at the bottom of the pile in the MGM lobby, met with Knight's attorney before the hearing but refused to speak with state prosecutors. He testified that Suge had nothing to do with his beating, contradicting statements the police said he made shortly after the assault. Whether he perjured himself or not, Lando kept well within game rules (ratting in such a public setting would do him no good in his circles). Despite Anderson's surprising testimony, the judge wasn't convinced of Suge's innocence and held him for three months of "diagnostic evaluation" before delivering the nine-year sentence.

Currently, local investigators are busy dredging up a 1995 case that had long since been settled out of court. The victim, Anthony Bell, a record promoter who worked for Puffy as well as Suge, was assaulted at a Death Row Christmas bash, allegedly because he wouldn't divulge Puffy's mother's address. Bell told investigators he was beaten with champagne bottles and forced to drink urine. If successfully prosecuted on this charge, Suge could be facing 25 years under L.A.'s new three-strike law—if the Feds or a fellow inmate doesn't get him first.

At press time, Suge Knight sat inside the L.A. County Jail's module 1700, awaiting transfer to a California state prison. He was still in protective custody on account of the many jailed gang members—Crip and Blood—looking to take his life. The price on his head is high. California law prohibits prisoners from running businesses while on lockdown, so Knight has to trust his associates to keep his company alive. Three days after Knight's sentencing, label spokesman George Pryce said, "It's business as usual at Death Row. Norris Anderson, who is general manager and Mr. Knight's brother-in-law, has been successfully running the company for the past five months. Until any further notice, he will remain at the helm." Days later, Pryce resigned.

One man still tending to Death Row's business is Suge's chief counsel, David Kenner, who's gone virtually unmentioned in all the speculation surrounding the label. That is, until February 13, when he was subpoenaed by Federal investigators to open Death Row's books. As a white, heavily connected lawyer standing behind the large black media target that is Suge Knight, Kenner may be the only major player in the Death Row camp to escape the current mess relatively unscathed.

A powerful man in L.A. law circles, Kenner first gained notoriety in 1988 when he defended Mafia-linked scam artist Barry Minkow in one of California's most notorious cases. Though he lost that and other

INCARCERATED DRUG KINGPIN MICHAEL HARRIS SENT A FORMAL COMPLAINT TO INTERSCOPE THAT CLAIMED HE WAS "AN ORIGINAL ORGANIZER, OWNER, AND SHARE-HOLDER" OF DEATH ROW RECORDS.

major cases, he's built a lucrative practice defending some of the country's most infamous drug lords. The 55-year-old Brooklyn-born family man and USC law graduate lives in the plush suburb of Encino, in a mansion surrounded by high fences and surveillance cameras. Former employees chuckle about the fully loaded Uzi he once kept sitting on a table in his home office. His running buddy, Tony Brooklier, is a well-respected criminal lawyer, who also happens to be the son of late mafioso Dominic Brooklier, onetime boss of La Cosa Nostra.

Known as a savvy backroom dealer, Kenner is the author of a number of contracts and agreements that have recently come under intense scrutiny. He drafted a strange two-page confession in which a Death Row accountant, Steve Cantrock, admitted to stealing $4.5 million from Suge Knight. Cantrock's associates told federal investigators that he was physically coerced into signing the document—an accusation Knight and Kenner have denied. Cantrock has since gone into hiding.

In the midst of Suge's probation hearings, it was revealed that Kenner was renting a house in Malibu from deputy DA Larry Longo, the prosecutor who initially oversaw Knight's probation. Suge ended up living in the house, and neighbors complained about his armed guards and late-night parties. Soon after, Longo's 18-year-old daughter, Gina, became the first white artist to sign with Death Row. The L.A. prosecutor's office has since suspended Longo indefinitely because of "the appearance of impropriety" in his relationship with Kenner and Knight.

Kenner's dealings with Longo are unusual to be sure, but even

more interesting is his association with Michael Harris (a.k.a. Harry-O), an incarcerated drug kingpin and member of the Bounty Hunter Bloods. Now serving a 28-year sentence at Lancaster State Prison for drug trafficking and attempted murder, Harris made a truckload of cash from the cocaine trade during the 1980s. "Harry-O is one of them niggas that was making like fifty million in the streets," said a former South Central resident. Harris invested his assets in a number of ventures: limo services, hair salons, a maintenance company, and *Checkmates,* a Broadway play starring Denzel Washington.

Kenner's relationship with Harris goes back to 1989 when he helped defend him and another big-time dealer in the Villabona drug ring case (in which massive amounts of cocaine were imported from Colombia). Harris lost the case but gained a business associate.

In an unfiled January 21, 1996, complaint that was sent to Interscope Records president Jimmy Iovine from Lancaster prison, Harris claims 50 percent of all of Death Row's proceeds. "Plaintiff Michael Harris," the document asserts, "was at all times mentioned herein, an original organizer, owner, and shareholder of a corporation known as Death Row Records, Inc. . . . " Harris says he met with Knight and Kenner in his jail cell on September 1, 1991, where they conceived the plan to form a company called Godfather Entertainment, Inc., of which Death Row Records would be a division. Harris would provide the overall "philosophy and direction" of the company as well as $1.5 million, while Knight would handle the day-to-day operations with Kenner's assistance.

Harris, who's been monitoring Death Row's troubles from his prison cell, seems none too pleased with the way his alleged investments have been handled. "David [Kenner] is a piece of work," he recently told a Fox News reporter. "The shit's about to hit the fan."

Whether or not Harry-O invested money in the Death Row venture, various documents suggest he was indeed connected to the company. A *Hollywood Reporter* story dated February 23, 1992, announced the launch of the new label Death Row, which would be run under the umbrella of "a new diversified media company, GF Entertainment (GFE)." In a March 2, 1992, filing with California's Secretary of State, the directors of GFE were listed as David Kenner and Lydia Harris, Michael Harris's wife. And in an April 15 filing with the L.A. county clerk, Death Row was registered under the umbrella corporation GF Music, Inc., with Kenner listed as Chairman of the Board of Directors.

Federal authorities are now investigating whether the funds used to start Death Row came from drug money, and if so, who knew about it. As former U.S. Strike Force attorney Marvin Rudnick told Fox's *Undercover* recently: "Anyone who is involved knowing that the profits from illegal activity, such as drug money, were being invested into a legitimate enterprise has the danger of facing either a grand jury or jail." In other words, if Harris's money was tainted and was the money used to launch Death Row, then anyone who knew this and still did business with the label could be facing racketeering charges.

Harris, it turns out, is not the only party claiming a piece of the Row. The same month that he drafted his complaint, Solar Records head Dick Griffey and former N.W.A songwriter the D.O.C. filed a $125 million suit against Death Row and Interscope, claiming they

GOOD KNIGHT?

Death Row CEO Suge Knight states his case to the judge and the community

On February 7, representatives of Death Row Records contacted VIBE to say that Suge Knight wanted to do an interview from prison. The exact date and time were to be arranged through his lawyer, David Kenner. "He's the man who can get you in," we were told. After a week of unreturned phone calls to Kenner's office, VIBE's Rob Marriott decided to go to the L.A. County Central Jail in hopes of meeting with Knight directly. In the visitors' waiting room he ran into Kenner. When he asked if the interview could happen that day, Kenner gave him a blank stare and said, "What interview?" That night, February 14, we received an anonymous message saying "Mr. Knight declines interview."

On February 28, just before he was sentenced to nine years in prison for probation violation for his role in an attack on Orlando Anderson the night of Tupac's shooting, Suge Knight made a fifteen-minute statement, excerpts from which follow:

I'm not here to try and sugarcoat my life and say I've been the most perfect guy in the world. But this is my life and I feel I should speak about my life.

I've learned a lot from being incarcerated. I've gotten closer to God and I've read the Bible inside out. I've learned that my role in the community is important as far as kids and the elders. I do a lot of good in the community and I don't do it for publicity or fame. The stuff I've done has come from my heart.

I know in the past, when I was working security in the music business, a few times I had fights. These were fights with my hands. I'm guilty for those fights, and I got punished for them.

When I walk through this courtroom, I see the DA say everybody hates me; I'm a bad guy; I'm this monster. And I don't see it. 'Cause if I was that type of person, these guys wouldn't keep following me around, coming to the studio wanting to work with me, coming to the jail to visit with me.

I'm not trying to be a politician. I believe in the community, 'cause that's all I've ever had. I've seen mayors, even the president, give speeches and say they gonna give back to the community, that they'll hire people from the community. And we never see it. When I was growing up, it never happened.

MAY 1997

So when—thanks to God—I was able to make a little money and do these things, I done them. But instead of someone giving me applause, they slandered my name. A few times I was treated like a wild animal. And the way you treat a wild animal is, you either catch him and hunt him down or throw him in a cage. Or kill him.

I've been in a cage for five months, where they feed me when they want to feed me, and they give me water when they feel I should have water. And I was this close to being dead, 'cause I still got the bullet in my head.

Being in prison has made me realize

I definitely don't want to do my life behind bars. But if it's more positive for the community by me being incarcerated, I'm willing to sacrifice. I'm willing to give my life for a friend or for kids. I really feel I'm more positive now.

I'd like to take out time to thank Dr. [C. DeLores] Tucker for coming down [to today's hearing]. It was a surprise because we always been on different sides of the fence. I know Dr. Tucker argued with me a lot about some of our lyrics; but I've made my own decision that any album I put out, the artist can never use the word "nigger." After being in County, I can't put out a record just to say anything anymore.

So I don't agree with all the things that's being brought against me right now as far as my reputation. I am a man, your honor, and I have a family and kids and loved ones. And I would like them to know the truth.

I been through a lot this year. I lost my best friend. A lot of people don't realize how it is to lose a best friend. I always wanted a little brother, and now he's not here.

Besides all that, I'm not mad, but I'm disappointed at Tupac's mother. While I'm incarcerated, people tell her that the songs I paid for and marketed is her songs. And she made statements saying that he never got any money. I got signed documents where he received

over $2.5 million, even before he was supposed to receive money. And beyond all that, when he was incarcerated, I gave his mother $3 million. But when the media gets it, it turns around that I left him for dead, I left him with zero, and that I'm this monster.

Whether it's my competition or prosecution, they made me look like Frankenstein. And if I look like Frankenstein, even though Frankenstein could be the nicest creature on earth, when he failed or when he died, everybody applauded. They clapped instead of cried.

And as far as the situation with the fight, I'm not trying to open up the case or go back to the incident in Vegas, but I wanna stipulate on that because it's important to me, 'cause I gotta live with this. When [Orlando] Anderson came up to testify, I'd be the first to say, he's not a friend of mine. And to be honest, I felt that this guy could play with the truth and go against me just to lie. But since he was under oath, I felt he told the truth.

Your honor, I was breakin' up the fight. I knew I was on probation. I put my freedom and my life on the line. And I feel if I wouldn't have stopped that fight—I'm not saying the same person who came and shot us later was these type of people, but if they was—instead of me getting shot in my head and one person dead, it could have been thirty people dead in Vegas at the MGM.

And even at the end, your honor, when everybody say "it was a

In his first few days in prison, Suge Knight confided in fellow convict _Sanyika Shakur_ (a.k.a. Monster Kody). Sanyika, now a free man, reveals what Suge told him really happened the night Tupac was shot.

WELCOME TO THE TERROR ZONE

DECEMBER 1997

been in these stoops since I was fifteen. This is what I said to Suge as we ambled down the massive central corridor at the California Institute for Men (CIM, or Chino) in Chino, California. He and I both had our hands cuffed behind our backs as we were escorted by two correctional officers with P-24 battle batons.

"Face the fucking wall," barked a jar-headed correctional officer in army fatigues. Prisoners who'd been traversing the corridor just prior to our exit from the Segregated Housing Unit edged closer to the yellow wall while stealing glimpses in our direction.

"Man," said Suge, swaggering in an attempt to look comfortable, "this shit is hectic."

Yeah, I responded, trailing behind his big frame. Welcome to the terror zone.

Constructed in 1941, Chino is not simply a prison but a complex of many prisons. A monument of razor wire and cinder block, it stands as one of the tightest maximum-security facilities in Southern California. The archaic cell blocks that extend from the central corridor stretch three tiers above the floor with as many as thirty-six cells to a tier. Each eight-foot-by-nine-foot cell holds two men for up to twenty-three hours a day.

On the east end of the corridor sits Palm Hall–or the Hole, as prisoners call it–CIM's answer to disciplinary problems and security risks. The guards in Palm Hall don't wear the usual uniform; they floss around the block in army-green jumpsuits, spear-proof flak jackets, and combat boots. As the guards' gear suggests, the Hole has seen its share of warfare. It was under all this concrete, steel, and animosity that I met Suge Knight.

I knew he'd be coming to Palm Hall perhaps even before he did. I reasoned that as a celebrity he'd be held in Involuntary Protective Custody (IPC)–just as Makaveli, then known as Tupac Shakur (no relation to me), was in 1995 at the Clinton Correctional Facility in Dannemora, New York. Before my honorable discharge from the Eight Tray Gangster Crips (when I was known as Monster Kody), I had run up a karmic debt myself–which I repaid during many years behind bars–but the poetic justice of Suge's fate seemed even more profound.

The last time I had seen Makaveli was in April of 1996 during the video shoot for the X-rated version of "How Do U Want It." I was on the run, about to go back to prison for a parole violation, and Makaveli was blowing up. But even then his stress was evident. We both had our demons.

After Makaveli was shot, I procured an avenue for news clippings to trickle in so I could keep up with the case. On hearing of his death, my first thought was that Suge had him set up. I had no evidence but had heard that a feud was brewing over contractual matters, including Makaveli's firing his lawyer, David Kenner, and his wanting to leave Death Row to start his own label. I read and reread all the news clippings about the shooting. Things kept fitting ill to me.

I'd read that he had no vest on and then saw a photo in VIBE to substantiate this fact. Yet in my experience, Makaveli went nowhere without a vest or his heat. And if his killers were the Southside Crips, with whom he'd supposedly fought that evening, why didn't the shooter dump on every car in the caravan? Suge's entourage was allegedly made up of top-ranking (Blood) Pirus, so why would a Crip pass up all those points to shoot someone who wasn't even a Blood? These thoughts ran through my head before I met the man.

In December 1996, Suge came to Palm Hall as I predicted. On top of his never having been in prison—despite his numerous convictions—Suge was staying in the Hole, where he would find it hard to breathe. I knew I'd be able to extract some inside information on Makaveli's shooting.

We'd never met on the streets. Although our sets don't get along, we never had any combat because of the distance between South Central and Compton. Besides, we were both in our thirties and had no time for red and blue rivalries. Out on the street, I'd heard that Suge was "on some Piru shit." But in here, neither his wealth nor my reputation mattered. We were equals, and that's how I approached him.

I knew that coming from L.A. County Jail he would have nothing. I wrote him a brief letter introducing myself and explaining the politics of the Hole. With the letter I included soap, deodorant, lotion, and a few Top Ramen soups. I put all of this in a big envelope and had it rushed to him. The next day he replied:

> A Monster,
> Good looking out. I wish we could hook up on the streets but it is never to [sic] late. My homeboy Poc [sic] had love for you so you know how it go if he had love for somebody I did too. He told me he would have been playing you in your life story. When the time is right we will talk.
>
> Suge

I couldn't believe it. This man was the CEO of a hundred-and-twenty-five-million-dollar company, yet his writing was no better, perhaps even worse, than my seven-year-old son's. Perhaps the brotha was just stressed out and wrote the letter in haste. I sent him a kite—a letter weighted with soap and tied to a long strip of bedsheet that gets delivered by being thrown from cell to cell—acknowledging receipt of his note and advising him to push the issue of going to general population. The following day he responded with a note that said I should let Death Row do the soundtrack for a movie about my life. The writing, like before, was in clumsy stick fashion.

I used some prison connections to get Suge and I put on the law-library list together. This way we'd be next to one another for at least three hours a week. I was a bit apprehensive preparing for our first meeting. After all, I'd seen men in and out of prison actually tremble when speaking about him.

Before our rendezvous I was stripped out to make sure I'd be unarmed. I'm sure Suge had to go through the same routine: Lift your arms up; stick out your tongue; pull back your ears; lift up your nut sack; bend at the waist; spread your cheeks and cough; lift your right foot; now your left. Any false teeth, dentures, or partials? You either complied or never came out of the cell. On went the cuffs, open came the door. When I reached the bottom of the stairs, I saw Suge facing the wall to my left. I eased over to him, noting his dimensions—six foot four, 330 pounds—in case things got out of hand.

"What's up, homie?" I was momentarily taken aback by his jovial greeting. I expected a harsher "I'm Suge Knight" type of response. I said I was well and just taking it one day at a time. We were escorted through two security doors and out into the law library, where we were put into gray, telephone booth–size cages. After the cages were secured with Yale padlocks, the handcuffs were removed. Suge was in his cage; I was in mine.

"Eh, Monster," he said, breaking the ice, "I heard Geronimo Pratt was here too?" I told Suge that Pratt left the same day Suge came; in fact, he had taken Geronimo's cell. It sort of irked me that he called me Monster after I had clearly signed each letter Sanyika. What if I used his banging name and called him Sugar Bear? I asked how he was doing so far.

"Man," he said, exhaling a tremendous amount of air, "this whole thing is a trip. I'm losing weight. I can't use no phone or get contact visits. And what's up with that tier they got me on? Fools be yelling and shit." Clearly, he was going through it. They had no shoes to fit him, so his man from VNG [Van Ness Gangsters] gave him some shower shoes. In return he gave the guy a photo of a half-naked woman taken at Makaveli's birthday party in Vegas. Suge's orange jumpsuit was two sizes too small. And on this day, he had only one side of his head shaved.

"Ain't that cold," he said when I asked about it. "The razor broke. I asked the police for another one, but they never came back. Plus, how I'm s'posed to shave and shower in ten minutes?"

Perhaps I'd been in these stoops too long. Most prisoners I knew could shower, shave, masturbate, and get their shoes on before the door opened again.

"I read your book," he said, "and seen you and your family on that documentary. Your moms is a strong woman." I thanked him for the compliment about Moms and then asked about Makaveli.

"That's my best friend," he said, speaking in present tense. "We go everywhere together." He started reminiscing about the wild times he and 'Pac had at Suge's Las Vegas nightclub. "We used to close up 662 at twelve, lock the doors, and give out free drinks and just get our freak on!"

How was my boy, though?

"He was the happiest he said he's ever been. Did you see the lowrider I got him?"

No, I hadn't seen it. Why all this talk about cars?

"Yeah, we got one just alike, 1961. He never drives it, though. I'm gonna get the engine and all that chromed up." Why would you have his car? I wanted to yell at him. And why would you still be working on it now? My mind was racing. So, y'all got some lo-lo's, huh? I asked, just to see where he'd go with it.

"Oh yeah, we got everything alike," Suge replied. "The Jags, the Bentleys. We even had the contest to see who could get the most women to tattoo our name on them." He chuckled at this for a long while.

When we met the following week, Suge's jumpsuit was fitting slightly looser. No sooner had we made it through the door than the library clerk named Reverend Stern started yapping. "Hey, I just saw you on the news this morning." Both Suge and I asked who.

"You," he answered, indicating Suge with a nod.

"Oh yeah?" said Suge, his voice indicating more concern than he intended.

"The DA says he's filing a three-strikes case against you for an old assault charge." To this Suge said nothing, and the silence became pregnant.

"Whatcha think about that?" asked Rev. Stern, leaning over a graffiti-scarred banister.

me that I could have all of his songs for thirty thousand dollars if I just got him out of jail? I told him naw, to keep his songs, but I'd get him out. He said he'd always wanted a rag Benz, so I got him one. Plus, I got his mother a house. I'll tell you this homie, God don't like ugly."

We'd all seen the black 500 droptop. And the house. Not one vehicle, however—not the Benz, the Jag, the Rolls, the Hummer, or the lo-lo—was in Makaveli's name. All the jewelry, the limo bills, and hotel accommodations were stacked against Makaveli like an advance. According to Suge, Makaveli left owing him—after sixty million dollars' worth of album sales in 1996 alone. Imagine that.

Impatient, I asked about the shooting.

"Earlier that day," Suge began in a solemn tone, "dude snatched a necklace with the Death Row coat of arms. 'Pac was upset about that. You know how he gets: when it's on, it's on. Then, later that night, 'Pac sees fool. So we touched him up a bit, you know. Still didn't get that necklace, though. Then we go on back to my spot, change, and hang out a bit; trying to find some freaks to come to the club. Tyson had won, and we was going to celebrate. 'Pac was trippin', though. All that day, he was talkin' 'bout how he never wanted to go back to prison. Never.

"Anyway, we rollin'; everything is tight. We talkin' 'bout this and that when all of a sudden, boom, boom, boom, boom! We start takin' heavy hits. I punch it; bust a U-turn, but I realize I got a flat. Then I

SUGE FELL SILENT, OVERWHELMED BY THE RUSH OF MEMORIES. I TOO WAS TRIPPIN' 'CAUSE I DIDN'T KNOW MAKAVELI WAS STILL TALKING AFTER THE SHOOTING. I ASKED, WHO SHOT TUPAC?

"That's nothing," replied Suge, his husky voice rising an octave. "Just the same old bullshit. I ain't worried. You know, it's like with this violation here: At first they said it was because I left the country. Then they said I had a dirty test. When that didn't work, they brought up the fight in Vegas. They just fuckin' with me."

The cage squeaked against his shifting body weight. The supposed third strike stemmed from the beating of a Bad Boy Records promoter at a 1995 Death Row Christmas party. The case was filed but never prosecuted. Now, all Suge's prior infractions were being reviewed.

I'd heard that Afeni, Makaveli's mom, had gotten a three-million-dollar royalty check from Interscope, so I asked about this. "Naw," Suge said with a tone of disgust. "I gave her that money. She got some lawyer who says he's been a friend of the family for twenty years, talkin' 'bout 'Pac had a bad contract. That's bullshit. When he was on Interscope, he was only gettin' four points. I got him eighteen points. And they talkin' 'bout he was cheated. 'Pac was happy. You seen all his jewelry, right?" I felt like Suge was changing the subject again.

"Monster, listen, when I went out to New York to see 'Pac, he was stressed out. He wanted to get out of prison. Don't you know, he told

see 'Pac is hit. But he still talkin', like it ain't nothing. My head was bleedin', and 'Pac said I should be the one sweatin' it 'cause I got shot in the head. Then the Vegas police come and draw down on us; they f'in to shoot us! We trying to tell 'em that we the victims, but they make us get down on the ground anyway."

He fell silent, as if overwhelmed by the rush of memories. I too was tripping 'cause I didn't know Makaveli was still talking after the shooting. Who shot him? I asked, feeling myself getting angry.

"You know who did it?" Suge said, grittin' his teeth. "Them niggas that's catchin' hell right now." I knew he was talking about the Southside Compton Crips. In the days following Makaveli's shooting, their 'hood was practically overrun by shooters. Yet his answer was insufficient, and I pressed again: Who specifically dumped, though?

"Baby Lane," he said, and exhaled. I assumed he meant Orlando Anderson, the Compton resident who'd already been named as a suspect in the shooting. By the end of our conversation, Suge's legendary bravado was gone. A humble respect descended over him that reminded me of a defeated man who'd lost his most prized possession in the game of life. For some of us, there just ain't no sunshine.

SHOOK ONE

DECEMBER 1997

He says he's neither a Crip nor a killer. In fact, he says he's a big Tupac fan. Orlando Anderson tells *Sanyika Shakur* what it's like to be accused of shooting your favorite rapper.

On the evening of September 7, 1996, after Mike Tyson's first-round knockout of Bruce Seldon, a melee broke out in the lobby of the MGM Grand Hotel in Las Vegas. The assailants were members of Death Row Records and the Mob Pirus (a Blood faction from Compton). Their target was 22-year-old Orlando Anderson, who is listed in LAPD files as a Southside Crip. Involved in the beatdown was none other than Tupac Shakur. Three hours later, Tupac and Suge took their last, fateful drive together down the Vegas Strip.

Within three weeks, a Compton police affidavit had named Anderson as the primary suspect in Tupac's shooting. On October 2, he was arrested on an unrelated murder warrant and questioned about the Shakur case, then released days later. Vegas police now say there's not enough evidence to prosecute him, but cops in Compton still consider him a suspect. This didn't stop Anderson from bringing suit on September 8, 1997, against the slain rapper's estate and Death Row for physical damages and "severe emotional and mental distress." Four days later, Afeni Shakur countersued for the wrongful death of her son.

Anderson and his lawyer, Renee L. Campbell, showed up two hours late for our interview. Dressed in a light plaid GUESS? shirt, baggy jeans, and new Jordans, his diamond earring glistening, Orlando sat across from me, clasping and unclasping his hands. His eyes were untrusting and skeptical, but also soft and questioning.

Why did the Death Row crew zero in on you that night at the MGM?

I really don't know why. I don't even know them.

Who pushed you first?

Actually, I think it was Tupac.

What did he say when he first stepped to you?

I don't really think they said anything. It happened so fast. All I felt was a swarm.

You didn't recognize nobody else? Did you recognize Suge?

I seen him on the videotape later.

Where we from in Compton, our first instinct—after being assaulted, insulted, shoe stepped on—is to respond. Did you feel like calling your peeps?

Me and my brother and them ain't like that. I was just scared because I done heard so much about these guys. It was, like, Damn, what did I do?

So you're not a Southside Crip?

No.

Are you affiliated with the Southside Crips?

No. I ain't no gang member. I know a lot of people; I grew up with a lot of people; I went to school with a lot of people.

So, nobody in your immediate family bangs?

My brothers? Naw.

Besides your brothers?

Well, y'knowhamsayin', there's my uncle and them.

The police said that they raided a Southside hangout, and there were guns there and a diploma on the wall with your name on it. Yet you said you lived next-door.

[Anderson's lawyer writes on a yellow notepad and pushes it toward him] I'm not gonna answer that.

Campbell: That affidavit is full of fiction. There is nothing in there that's independently corroborated. We don't know why that particular Compton police officer wrote it, but it was full of lies.

It was reported that you were bragging about whacking Makaveli.

You might as well don't even pay attention to the affidavit.

That wasn't just in the affidavit. People on the street in Compton told VIBE you were bragging about it.

[Shakes his head; no response]

Do they call you Baby Lane?

Some people call me that.

When I was in jail with Suge Knight, he said, "Baby Lane did it." How do you respond to this guy's saying you were the shooter?

I really don't know why Suge would say something like that. I don't even know Suge.

Campbell: As far as we're concerned, whatever Suge Knight is saying, he's saying for his own gain. We've also named him in the lawsuit. There's no evidence against Orlando. If they would do a proper investigation, they would very likely find who killed Tupac.

On the stand, you said Suge was not involved in your beating, that he tried to stop it. Now you're naming him in the lawsuit for participating in your beating.

At the time, I was fearing for my life.

You were fearing Suge's camp? Death Row people?

Campbell: We don't want to comment on whom he was fearing.

Aren't you worried about perjury charges?

Campbell: Even at the time [Orlando] testified, the judge was very skeptical. People say what they need to say if their safety is threatened.

Why change the story now? Are you less scared?

Campbell: No, it's not that. Orlando was advised by his lawyers that if he was going to bring this lawsuit, then he would need to bring it now. He suffered injuries; he has damages that he wants to collect on.

Anderson: I was kicked in my head, and I was bleeding out of my ear. My hands right here were real swollen.

How do you feel about Tupac's mother filing this countersuit against you?

That's nonsense to me.

Campbell: That was done solely in response to the lawsuit we filed. Her lawsuit has absolutely no basis.

You were on America's Most Wanted. *Have you had any troubles because you were named as a suspect in Tupac's killing?*

I've been threatened a lot.

How has this altered your life?

I just stay in the house all the time.

Why don't you just get vested and heated and continue to do your thing? Life goes on. Even 'Pac himself said it.

I ain't that type of person. I'll just put it in the Lord's hands.

Did anybody ever tell you that you very much resemble Tupac?

Yeah, a couple of people have told me that.

Do you feel any resentment toward Tupac's spirit, like, Look at what the hell you done got me into?

I think like that all the time, wondering why. Not only put me through a lot of stuff but put my family through a lot of stuff too.

So, have you lost passion for Tupac's music? Do you still listen to him?

Yeah, I still listen to his music.

Because you feel him?

Yeah. To me, he was like the Marvin Gaye of rap. If he was to come out with some new music, I'm still about his music.

Do you have a favorite 'Pac song?

"All Eyez on Me."

Especially now, huh? What do you wish at this particular juncture in your life?

I wish they would find who did it so I can prove my innocence.

When Tupac Shakur died, in 1996, he didn't need an obituary. His archive of start-some-shit soliloquies, ghetto ballads, and odes to various revolutions thoroughly recounted the artist's turbulent life and even foreshadowed his demise. Now, under the watchful eye of Tupac's mother, Afeni Shakur–who sued Death Row Records for control of hundreds of unreleased songs, which she culled to produce the double CD *R U Still Down? (Remember Me)*–hip hop's complex crown prince is given new voice.

This 24-track retrospective, recorded between 1991 and 1994, is far from being 2Pac's greatest work; an unnerving sense of déjà vu permeates the sprawling opus. For example, "When I Get Free," sans the countrified twang, sounds like 1992's "Soulja's Story" revisited and is resonant with the latter's warbled voice distortions. "Thug Style," one of the record's few stellar moments, is neverthe-less reminiscent of 1995's "Old School," in which Shakur articulates his East Coast conception while basking in California love. Like 'Pac's erstwhile Digital Underground homies once surmised, on this album it's mostly the same song. Hidden in the mire, however, are the intoxicating fuck you–isms of "Lie to Kick It" and the lovelorn lament of "Do for Love," proof positive that 2Pac was sharpest when his subject matter got around.

Although the production (courtesy of Mike Mosley, Warren G, Johnny "J," and others) is a bit dated, it's the 2Pac of the '90–'91 DU era that com-mands attention. Riding the party-hearty sounds of Parliament's 1977 "Flash Light," the lively "Let Them Thangs Go" provides temporary relief from the fatalistic aura of Shakur's later work. But the fun doesn't last; instead, there's much gruesome irony. "I keep my finger on the trigger 'cuz a nigga's tryin' to kill me," 'Pac screams in the scathing "Hellrazor." The truth hurts.

Too bad 2Pac wasn't around to regulate this project, because if he was, *R U* would probably have been an excellent EP instead of an LP-squared. Either way, remember him we will.

Gabriel Alvarez

(REMEMBER ME)

R U STILL DOWN?

FEBRUARY 1998

AMARU/JIVE

HOLLER IF YA SEE ME

Living in Detroit has its advantages when it comes to understanding the souls of black folk. No industry; no popular gossip jocks like Wendy Williams or the Baka Boyz. So hip hop fans have to freestyle when it comes to news and information.

If we are to believe what we hear at local barbershops, nail salons, and topless bars, then Tupac, his family, and some presumably well-paid, official-looking stand-ins have conspired to pull the ultimate scam. There's no fooling my homies: Tupac is still alive.

There are variations on this theme, obviously, but for brothers and sisters across the country, there's room for reasonable doubt:

Well, tell me this: Why would his mama cremate him so quickly?

I heard he wanted to get off Death Row, so he shook Suge. Shiiiit.

That nigga Machiavelli did the same thing: faked his death to fool his enemies.

He was gonna have to go back to jail in New York if he lost his appeal. He wasn't tryin' to have that.

Ain't you ever wanted to act like you was dead, peep your funeral, see who was really crying? That's what he's doing: laying in the cut, weeding out the haters.

Sure, it's postmortem denial, amplified by the lack of any formal funeral service. Tupac was so full of life, even while he was obsessed with dying, that it's hard to believe he's actually gone. On a certain level, we need him—our fearless trickster, able to take five bullets, shoot up crooked white cops, and walk away. To accept that he's dead is not only to admit his mortality but also to acknowledge that the real nigga myth—made three-dimensional in Tupac—is vulnerable.

If Zora were still trekking backwoods (today they'd be postindustrial ghettos), searching for our essence, I have no doubt she'd add the speculation around 'Pac's death to her collection of Br'er Rabbit–like tall tales. These improvisational fables of burrowing underground serve as symbolic resistance and, at least in Tupac's case, as a way of coping with loss by breathing life into his legacy.

'Pac, if you readin' this, keep bangin'. I see you, baby.

dream hampton

AFTERWORDS

John Singleton

It is very difficult to express what I'm feeling at this moment. Here in Los Angeles on 92.3 The Beat, I hear many people expressing their shock, surprise, and hurt, all at the loss of Tupac. I'm sitting here feeling all that and more. Am I shocked? Yes. Am I hurt? Yes. Am I surprised? No. For years I've felt that something like this could happen to Pac. But now that he's gone, I'm feeling very numb.

When I saw *Juice*, Tupac's performance jumped out at me like a tiger. My favorite scene is the one where he threatens Omar Epps at the locker: "You right, I am crazy. I don't care about you, I don't care about myself." The scene felt so real. Here was an actor who could portray the ultimate crazy nigga. A brother who could embody the freedom that an "I don't give a fuck" mentality gives a black man. I thought this was some serious acting. Maybe I was wrong.

For many, it is easy to write Pac off as a crazy nigga who didn't know reality from stage or screen. It is true that he was an actor in every sense of the word. Tupac's acting career began at the age of 12 in *A Raisin in the Sun* at the Baltimore School for the Arts. He possessed a natural gift for acting. Pac had aspirations to be as good or better than De Niro or Pacino. And I wanted to help him get there, to be his Scorsese. When I decided to cast him opposite Janet Jackson in *Poetic Justice*, it was not without some problems.

During the filming of *Poetic Justice*, Pac both rebelled and accepted my attitude toward him as director/advisor. This was our dance in life and work. We'd argue, then make up. Get pissed off and then reconcile. This was the Tupac I knew: constantly traveling in his mind around what was right or wrong. Looking for a father figure. Searching to define himself as a black man who came from nothing and suddenly had it all—money, women, cars, jewelry, and fame.

Now that he's gone, I can only wonder what he'd feel to know that so many people are affected by his passing. Everyone has a different story about what he meant to them—good and bad. But Tupac spoke from a position that cannot be totally appreciated unless you understand the pathos of being a nigga—that is, a displaced African soul, full of power, pain, and passion, with no focus or direction for all that energy except his art.

Chuck D

Interviewed by Rob Kenner the weekend of Tupac's death

To me he's like the James Dean of our times. Basically a rebel without a cause. And the industry and the media are partially responsible for whatever goes down, in accenting on the negative aspect of a black celebrity. It's the soup-up, gas-up treatment. They soup him up and they're not there on the downside. People think that this man's life was entertainment.

One of our best talents is gone over some bullshit. I'm fuckin' pissed. I ain't putting up tears. Tears ain't doing a damn thing. Interscope will go on to sell 10 million copies of this album. Make a scholarship fund out of their share of the money. That's what I call making things happen.

Then, as of November 25, Chuck revised his opinion, and came to believe that Tupac might have faked his own death only to reappear in some foreign country. At a press conference in Atlanta, Chuck shared some of the reasons why he believes this theory.

Tupac was a reader of Nicolo Machiavelli, author of *The Prince*. [Shakur even adapted the name for his *Killuminati* album.] This Italian author and theorist is famous for faking his own death to fool his enemies, something Shakur apparently also talked of doing.

Tupac died on Friday the 13th.

Tupac was cremated so soon after his death.

Neither the suspects nor the white Cadillac they drove was ever found.

Tupac always wore a bulletproof vest, except this one time.

Las Vegas is "payoff city."

Death Row records had a lot to gain, with material for three albums unreleased.

Tupac's final album cover art depicts the artist in the image of Jesus Christ on the cross, possibly setting up his future resurrection.

Suge Knight and Tupac are the only two people with the guts and a high enough profile to pull off a stunt like this.

Ernest Dickerson

Interview by Andréa M. Duncan

Ernest Dickerson directed the film *Juice*, the gripping urban drama that launched Tupac Shakur's movie career. About a week after Shakur's death, Dickerson shared his memories and impressions with VIBE:

Tupac was a brilliant artist. The people who are saying negative things about him and gangsta rap are obviously people who didn't know him. But I knew him as an extremely sensitive, gentle soul who was very nurturing. I was impressed with his sensibility. His mind was constantly working, always putting that nervous energy into his work. Once he had gotten into character, he started working right away on his new album. He would sit in the corner and write.

He didn't even audition for the role of Bishop, he just came in and blew everyone away. He was hanging out with Treach [of Naughty By Nature; another actor in *Juice*] on the set, and we asked him what he was doing, and he said "Nothin'." We said, Why don't you read for the part, and he said, "OK, sure." and then he got up there and blew everyone else out of the water.

I feel very proud that we helped him get his start. I was praying for him when he got shot, and when I found out he had died I was devastated. He really liked people, and he liked to be liked by people. Perhaps his biggest fault was that he wanted to like people too much. He was very open and he never dismissed people, so he was a target for opportunists. He had enormous talent, and, unfortunately, I feel his best work was still ahead of him. The saddest part about this is that no one will ever know what he might have become.

The troubled, triumphant, tragic times of Tupac Shakur

SEPTEMBER 1968: Tupac's mother, Afeni Shakur, joins the New York Black Panther party at age 22.

APRIL 1969: Afeni is arrested and charged with conspiracy to bomb several public areas in New York City. While out on bail, Afeni courts two men: Legs, a local hood, and Billy, a member of the party.

SEPTEMBER 1983: Afeni enrolls 12-year-old Tupac in the 127th Street Ensemble, a Harlem theater group. In his first performance, Tupac plays Travis in *A Raisin in the Sun.*

JUNE 1986: Shakur's family moves to Baltimore. As MC New York, Tupac writes his first rap.

SEPTEMBER 1986: Tupac enrolls at the Baltimore School for the Arts, where he studies ballet and acting.

JUNE 1988: Tupac and his family move to Marin City,

a $10 million lawsuit against the Oakland police for alleged brutality following an arrest for jaywalking.

JANUARY 17, 1992: Tupac makes his big-screen debut in Ernest Dickerson's *Juice,* earning praise for his portrayal of Bishop. He is perhaps best remembered for the line "I am crazy. And I don't give a fuck!"

APRIL 11, 1992: Ronald Ray Howard, 19, shoots a Texas trooper. Howard's attorney claims *2Pacalypse Now,* which was in his client's tape deck, incited him to kill.

APRIL 5, 1993: Tupac is arrested in Lansing, Michigan, for taking a swing at a local rapper with a baseball bat during a concert. He's sentenced to ten days in jail.

JULY 23, 1993: John Singleton's *Poetic Justice,* starring Tupac and Janet Jackson, is released. Before filming began, Jackson demanded Shakur take an HIV test before she would do any kissing scenes.

OCTOBER 31, 1993: Tupac is arrested for allegedly shooting two off-duty Atlanta police officers who he says

LIVED FAST,

FEBRUARY 1971: Afeni, pregnant with Tupac, has her bail revoked; she's sent to the Women's House of Detention in Greenwich Village.

JUNE 16, 1971: Shortly after his mom is acquitted on bombing charges, Tupac Amaru Shakur is born in New York. *Tupac Amaru* are Inca words meaning "shining serpent." *Shakur* is Arabic for "thankful to God."

1975–1983: Tupac's family shuttles between the Bronx and Harlem, at times living in shelters.

1983: Legs comes to live with the Shakur family; Tupac "claims" him as his father. Legs introduces Afeni to crack.

California. "Leaving that school affected me so much," he said later. "I see that as the point where I got off track." Shortly after, Tupac moves in with a neighbor and begins selling drugs.

AUGUST 1988: Mutulu Shakur, Tupac's stepfather, is sentenced to sixty years in prison for his involvement in a 1981 armored-car robbery.

1990: Tupac joins Digital Underground as a roadie/dancer/rapper. While on tour, he learns that his mother is using crack.

JANUARY 3, 1991: Tupac makes his recording debut on DU's *This Is an E.P. Release.*

NOVEMBER 12, 1991: *2Pacalypse Now* is released. Shortly thereafter, Tupac files

AUGUST 22, 1992: Tupac has an altercation with old acquaintances in Marin City. A 6-year-old bystander is shot in the head. Tupac's half brother, Maurice Harding, is arrested but released due to lack of evidence.

SEPTEMBER 22, 1992: Tupac is denounced by Vice President Dan Quayle, who says *2Pacalypse Now* "has no place in our society."

FEBRUARY 1, 1993: *Strictly 4 My N.I.G.G.A.Z.* is released and eventually goes platinum.

MARCH 13, 1993: Tupac has a fight with a limo driver in Hollywood who accuses him of using drugs in the car. Tupac's arrested, but the charges are dropped.

were harassing a black motorist. Charges are eventually dropped.

NOVEMBER 18, 1993: A 19-year-old woman, whom Tupac picked up four days earlier in a New York nightclub, is allegedly sodomized and sexually abused by the rapper and three friends.

DECEMBER 1993: John Singleton is forced by Columbia Pictures to drop the rapper from the cast of his upcoming film, *Higher Learning.*

MARCH 10, 1994: Tupac is sentenced to fifteen days in a Los Angeles jail for punching out director Allen Hughes. (Hughes and his brother, Albert, had dropped Tupac from *Menace II Society.*)

MARCH 23, 1994: Tupac stars as Birdie, a troubled drug dealer, in *Above the Rim.* The soundtrack album, featuring the song "Pour Out a Little Liquor," recorded by Tupac's group, Thug Life, sells two million copies.

SEPTEMBER 7, 1994: Two Milwaukee teens murder a police officer and cite Tupac's "Souljah's Story" as their inspiration.

NOVEMBER 30, 1994: While on trial for sex and weapons charges, Tupac is shot five times and robbed of $40,000 worth of jewelry in the lobby

APRIL 1995: In a VIBE interview from jail, Tupac renounces his "Thug Life" persona and commits himself to positive works. He also implicates Biggie Smalls, Puffy Combs, Andre Harrell, his close friend Stretch, and others in the recording studio ambush.

AUGUST 1995: Biggie, Puffy, and Harrell tell VIBE they had no connection to Tupac's shooting.

OCTOBER 1995: Death Row Records CEO Suge Knight posts $1.4 million bond to release Tupac, who immedi-

APRIL 25, 1996: *All Eyez on Me* goes quintuple platinum.

MAY 1996: Tupac and Snoop Doggy Dogg release "2 of Americaz Most Wanted." In the video, caricatures of Biggie and Puffy are punished for setting up Tupac.

JUNE 4, 1996: Death Row releases Tupac's "Hit 'Em Up," a brutal diatribe against Biggie, Bad Boy, Mobb Deep, and others.

SEPTEMBER 4, 1996: Tupac returns to New York for the MTV Music Video Awards and gets into a scuffle.

FRIDAY, SEPTEMBER 13, 1996: After six days in critical condition, Tupac Shakur is pronounced dead at 4:03 P.M. His body is later cremated. He was 25.

NOVEMBER 5, 1996: Makaveli album, *The Don Killuminati: The 7 Day Theory*, released.

FEBRUARY 28, 1997: Suge Knight is sentenced to nine years in prison for his role in an attack on Orlando Anderson the night of Tupac's shooting.

MARCH 9, 1997: The Notorious B.I.G. (Christopher

DIED YOUNG

of a Times Square recording studio. Tupac checks himself out of the hospital less than three hours after surgery. The case remains unsolved.

DECEMBER 1, 1994: Tupac is acquitted of sodomy and weapons charges but is found guilty of sexual abuse.

FEBRUARY 14, 1995: Tupac is sentenced to up to four-and-a-half years and immediately begins serving his jail time in New York's Rikers Island penitentiary.

APRIL 1, 1995: While he's incarcerated, Tupac's third album, *Me Against the World,* debuts at No. 1 on *Billboard*'s pop chart. Fueled by the single "Dear Mama," the album goes double platinum in seven months.

ately flies to L.A., signs with Death Row, and begins recording *All Eyez on Me.*

NOVEMBER 30, 1995: Exactly one year after Tupac's shooting, Randy "Stretch" Walker is murdered execution-style in Queens.

FEBRUARY 1996: In VIBE, Tupac suggests he's been sleeping with Biggie's wife, Faith Evans. Faith denies the stories.

FEBRUARY 13, 1996: Tupac's Death Row debut, *All Eyez on Me*—rap's first double CD—is released.

MARCH 29, 1996: Words are exchanged and a gun is pulled when Death Row and Bad Boy employees face off after the *Soul Train* awards in Los Angeles.

SEPTEMBER 7, 1996: After leaving the Mike Tyson–Bruce Seldon fight in Las Vegas in Suge Knight's car, Shakur is shot four times in the chest by an assailant in a white Cadillac. Knight, who has connections with the Bloods, escapes with a minor injury. Shakur is rushed to University Medical Center, where he undergoes surgery, including the removal of his right lung.

SEPTEMBER 11, 1996: A Compton man who police say is associated with the L.A. Crips is shot to death while sitting in his car, the first in a series of gang-related murders. Police begin investigating possible connections to Tupac's shooting.

Wallace) is murdered in Los Angeles in a drive-by shooting.

OCTOBER 8, 1997: *Gang Related,* co-starring Tupac and James Belushi, is released. Nine days later, the soundtrack, which includes four Tupac songs, comes out on Death Row.

NOVEMBER 25, 1997: *R U Still Down? (Remember Me),* a double CD of previously unreleased Tupac tracks, comes out on Amaru Records, a label established to be run by Afeni Shakur.

MAY 29, 1998: Orlando Anderson is killed during a dispute at a Los Angeles car wash.

DISCOGRAPHY

Digital Underground
THIS IS AN E.P. RELEASE
TOMMY BOY RECORDS

Released January 3, 1991
Highest Chart Position:
#7 R&B, #29 Pop
Certified gold March 18, 1991
Tupac's recording debut on
the track "Same Song"

2PACALYPSE NOW
INTERSCOPE RECORDS

Released November 12, 1991
Highest Chart Position:
#13 R&B, #64 Pop
Certified gold April 19, 1995

STRICTLY 4 MY N.I.G.G.A.Z.
INTERSCOPE RECORDS

Released February 1, 1993
Highest Chart Position:
#4 R&B, #24 Pop
Certified platinum April 19,
1995

POETIC JUSTICE
soundtrack
EPIC RECORDS

Released June 28, 1993
Highest Chart Position:
#3 R&B, #23 Pop
Certified gold August 25, 1993
Contains 2Pac's "Definition of
a Thug Nigga"

ABOVE THE RIM
soundtrack
DEATH ROW RECORDS

Released March 7, 1994
Highest Chart Position:
#1 R&B, #2 Pop
Certified double platinum
August 31, 1994
Contains Thug Life's "Pour
Out a Little Liquor"

THUG LIFE, Volume 1
INTERSCOPE RECORDS

Released September 26, 1994
Highest Chart Position:
#6 R&B, #42 Pop
Certified gold January 24,
1996

ME AGAINST THE WORLD
INTERSCOPE RECORDS

Released February 27, 1995
Highest Chart Position:
#1 R&B, #1 Pop
Certified double platinum
December 6, 1995

ONE MILLION STRONG: THE ALBUM
MERGELA RECORDS

Released October 15, 1995
Highest Chart Position:
#36 R&B
Contains "Runnin'," featuring
2Pac, the Notorious B.I.G.,
and Stretch, which peaked at
#84 on the Pop Singles Chart,
#62 on the R&B Singles Chart,
and #14 on the Rap Singles
Chart

ALL EYEZ ON ME
DEATH ROW RECORDS

Released February 13, 1996
Highest Chart Position:
#1 R&B, #1 Pop
Certified seven times platinum
December 9, 1996

Makaveli
THE DON KILLUMINATI: THE 7 DAY THEORY
DEATH ROW RECORDS

Released November 5, 1996
Highest Chart Position:
#1 R&B, #1 Pop
Certified triple platinum
April 16, 1997

DEATH ROW'S GREATEST HITS
DEATH ROW RECORDS

Released November 19, 1996
Highest Chart Position:
#15 R&B, #35 Pop
Contains "Keep Ya Head Up,"
"Dear Mama," "Me Against the
World," "I Get Around," "Pour
Out a Little Liquor" (performed
by Thug Life), "Smile for Me
Now," and "Hit 'Em Up"
(which was initially released
June 4, 1996, on the "How Do
U Want It" maxi-single)

GRIDLOCK'D
soundtrack
DEATH ROW RECORDS

Released January 28, 1997
Highest Chart Position:
#1 R&B, #1 Pop
Contains "Wanted Dead or
Alive" (performed by 2Pac and
Snoop Doggy Dogg), "Never
Had a Friend Like Me" (per-
formed by 2Pac), and "Out the
Moon" (performed by Snoop
Doggy Dogg, featuring 2Pac,
Tray Deee, and Priest
"Soopafly" Brooks)
Certified gold April 16, 1997

GANG RELATED
soundtrack
DEATH ROW RECORDS

Released October 17, 1997
Highest Chart Position:
#1 R&B, #2 Pop
Contains "Life's So Hard,"
"Staring Through My Rear
Views," "My Niggaz," and
"Lost Souls"
Certified double platinum
November 13, 1997

R U STILL DOWN? (REMEMBER ME)
AMARU/JIVE RECORDS

Released November 25, 1997
Highest Chart Position:
#1 R&B, #2 Pop
Certified four times platinum
December 15, 1997

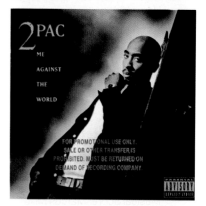

FILMOGRAPHY

JUICE

Release date: January 17, 1992
Director: Ernest R. Dickerson
Writers: Gerard Brown and Ernest R. Dickerson
Musical Score: Bomb Squad
Available on: Paramount Home Video
Length: 95m
Rating: R
Box office sales: $20.15 million
Cast: Omar Epps, Tupac Shakur (Bishop), Jermaine Hopkins, Khalil Kain, Cindy Herron, Vincent Laresca, Samuel L. Jackson

POETIC JUSTICE

Release date: July 23, 1993
Director: John Singleton
Writer: John Singleton
Musical Score: Stanley Clarke
Studio: Columbia TriStar Motion Picture Companies
Available on: Columbia TriStar Home Video and Baker & Taylor Home Video
Length: 109m
Rating: R
Box office sales: $27.5 million
Cast: Janet Jackson, Tupac Shakur (Lucky), Tyra Ferrell, Regina King, Joe Torry, Maya Angelou, Tone Loc, Q-Tip, Keith Washington

ABOVE THE RIM

Release date: March 23, 1994
Director: Jeff Pollack
Writer: Jeff Pollack
Musical Score: Marcus Miller
Studio: New Line Cinema
Available on: New Line Home Video
Length: 97m
Rating: R
Box office sales: $16.19 million
Cast: Duane Martin, Tupac Shakur (Birdie), Leon, Marlon Wayans, Tonya Pinkins, Bernie Mac

BULLET

Release date: January 21, 1997
Director: Julien Temple
Writers: Bruce Rubenstein and Sir Eddie Cook
Studio: New Line Home Video
Available on: New Line Home Video
Length: 96m
Cast: Mickey Rourke, Tupac Shakur (Tank), Ted Levine, Adrien Brody

GRIDLOCK'D

Release date: January 29, 1997
Director: Vondie Curtis Hall
Writer: Vondie Curtis Hall
Studio: Gramercy Pictures
Musical Score: Stewart Copeland
Length: 91m
Rating: R
Cast: Tim Roth, Tupac Shakur (Spoon), Thandie Newton

GANG RELATED

Release date: October 8, 1997
Director: Jim Kouf
Writer: Jim Kouf
Studio: Orion Pictures
Cast: James Belushi, Tupac Shakur (Rodriguez), Lela Rochon, Dennis Quaid

CONTRIBUTORS

GABRIEL ALVAREZ is the managing editor of *ego trip,* the arrogant voice of musical truth. He is the former senior editor of *RapPages* and is a contributor to both VIBE and *The Source.*

DAVID BRY, a Jersey Shore native, is an associate editor at VIBE. A 1995 graduate of Connecticut College, he lives in Manhattan and is an associate editor at *ego trip* magazine.

CHAIRMAN MAO, a longtime vinyl junkie and DJ, originally began writing about music in order to gain access to free records. In addition to VIBE, he regularly contributes to *The Source* and *Rap Pages,* and is editor-in-chief at *ego trip* magazine. In between wedding and bar mitzvah gigs, Mao cohosts the acclaimed vintage soul and funk radio program *Across 110th Street* on WKCR in New York City.

CHEO HODARI COKER is a freelance writer. His profiles, essays, and reviews have appeared in VIBE, *Rolling Stone, Essence,* the *Village Voice,* and numerous other publications.

ELLEN FANNING is the former art director at VIBE.

KAREN R. GOOD is a writer-at-large at VIBE. A native of Prairie View, Texas, Karen has written for and worked at *People* and *Seventeen* magazines. In addition, she has freelanced for various publications, including *Essence, The New York Times Magazine, Rap Pages, ego trip, Brooklyn Bridge,* and the *Village Voice.*

DREAM HAMPTON is a freelance writer. She lives in Detroit.

LARRY "THE BLACKSPOT" HESTER began his writing career as an aspiring rapper at the age of 13. A native of

Brooklyn, New York, he pursued a career in rap for several years until he found hip hop journalism more compelling. Presently, he is the music editor for *XXL* magazine. He is also the U.S. correspondent for the rap radio show on the UK's *Choice FM,* and has developed his own management company called Undadog Entertainment.

CORY JOHNSON is an editor at the on-line financial publication *thestreet.com.* He is a former senior editor at VIBE and the former editor of *Slam.*

ALAN LIGHT is an editor-at-large at VIBE. He was previously the magazine's editor-in-chief, founding music editor, and is a former senior writer for *Rolling Stone.*

OJ LIMA is the music editor at *Seventeen* magazine. A former VIBE staffer, he was born and raised in Providence, Rhode Island. He earned a B.A. in English from the University of Pennsylvania, and an M.A. in education from Columbia University Teachers College. Currently, he is working on a novel about the struggles of a young trumpet player.

ROBERT MARRIOTT is a Brooklyn-born journalist now living in the South Bronx. He began his writing career at the *Village Voice* at age 18. A former editor at *The Source,* he has written for several periodicals, including *Spin, ego trip,* and *Essence.* He writes a hip hop column for *Tower Pulse!* and speaks regularly at high schools and universities on the subject of hip hop and mythology. He is presently a consultant for an upcoming documentary of the life of Tupac Shakur, *Last Man on Earth.*

JOAN MORGAN is a freelance writer living in Brooklyn and a former VIBE staff writer.

GEORGE PITTS is picture editor at VIBE. He is a former assistant picture editor at *Entertainment Weekly.*

KEVIN POWELL is a freelance writer living in Brooklyn. A former VIBE senior writer and a frequent contributor to *Rolling Stone,* he is the author of *represent* (readers & writers press).

ALLISON SAMUELS works in *Newsweek*'s Los Angeles bureau.

SANYIKA SHAKUR, known as Monster Kody in his Crip days, is a California native and *RapPages* columnist. Shakur (no relation to Tupac) is the author of 1993's best-selling *Monster: The Autobiography of an L.A. Gang Member* (Atlantic Monthly Press).

DANYEL SMITH is the editor-in-chief of VIBE and a former rhythm and blues editor at *Billboard.* She has written for the *New York Times* and has been a columnist at *Spin.* Her work has also appeared in *Time, The New Yorker, Rolling Stone,* and the *Village Voice.* A California native, Danyel was music editor at *San Francisco Weekly* and a columnist at the *San Francisco Bay Guardian.* Danyel has just finished a year at Northwestern University as a 1996–97 National Arts Journalism Fellow.

JOSEPH V. TIRELLA is a reporter at *People* magazine. A former VIBE staffer, his writing has also appeared in *Slam.*

JOSH TYRANGIEL is a graduate student in American studies at Yale University. A former VIBE staffer, as a writer/producer for MTV News, he conducted the last television interview with Tupac Shakur.

CREDITS

Grateful acknowledgment is made to the following for permission to reprint photographs contained in *Tupac Shakur:*

Dina Alfano, page 127 • AP/Wide World Photos, pages 24, 26, 58, 61, 139 • Fitzroy Barrett/Globe Photos, Inc., page 82 (bottom right) • Michael Benabib, pages 66, 82 (top), 110 • Danny Clinch/ Outline, pages 23, 32, 140, 148 • Corjuni/ Outline, page 116 • Nicola Goode, page 14 • Rose Hartman/Globe Photos, Inc., pages 85 (top left), 153 • Bill Jones, pages 92, 100, 102 • Kelly Jordan/South Beach Photo Agency, pages 85 (center), 86 • David LaChapelle, Inc., pages 7, 104, 107 • Jay Lash, page 90 • Dana Lixenberg, pages 14, 68, 96, 99, 128 • Maurice McInnis, page 146 (top) • Gary Miller/Globe Photos, page 40 • Michael Miller, pages 35, 36, 95 • Yishai Minkin, page 12 • Shawn Mortensen, pages 10, 20 • Jeffrey Newbury/Outline, pages 28, 42, 130 • Norman Ng for Edie Baskin/Outline, page 3 • Michael O'Neill/Outline, pages 64, 70, 81 • Darby Orris/ LGI Photo Agency, page 55 • Ernie Paniccioli, pages 30, 84 (bottom left) • Malcolm Payne, page 117 • Matthew Pearson, Jr./DIVA DONE! Photos, pages 56, 57, 82 (bottom left), 83 (top left, top right, bottom left, bottom right), 84 (top left, top right, center, bottom right), 85 (top right), 124 • Al Pereira, pages 2, 38, 146 (bottom) • Photofest, page 141 • Karla Radford, page 138 • Eli Reed/ Columbia Pictures, page 141 • Reisig & Taylor Photography, pages 44, 49, 52, 62, 78, 136, 151 • Andrea Renault/Globe Photos, Inc., page 89 • Lisa Rose/ Globe Photos, Inc., page 83 (top center) • Lady Pink and Smith; photographed by Sue Schaffner, page 145 • Robert Spencer/Retna Ltd., page 141 • Mpozi Tolbert, pages 118 (top and bottom), 119 (top and bottom), 120, 121, 123 • Leon Walker, pages 75, 85 (bottom) • Dan Winters, pages 8, 9, 160 • Barbara Wüllenweber, page 114

I believe that everything you do bad comes back to you. So everything that I do that's bad, I'm going to suffer for it. But in my heart, I believe what I'm doing is right. So I feel like I'm going to heaven.